Pál Békésy

Tale Travellers

Pál Békésy

Tale Travellers

Illustrated by Judit Eszter Barna

ISBN 978-615-01-9278-9

Layout and book design: János Békésy

Contents

Day One

Mum opened the car door and put Pete and Judy in the kids' seat. She fastened the safety belts then got in the car too. As she was driving, she looked back in the review mirror and smiled to herself.

"You know, we're going to spend the next ten days at Pop, don't you? He can't wait for us to arrive."

"Of course we know," said Pete, turning towards Mum. "Dad is coming after us?"

"Not this time, honey, he has to work. But we'll have a separate holiday together, all of us."

"But you will still tell stories in the evenings, right?"

"Of course. But who knows, maybe this time Pop will be the storyteller," smiled Mum.

"Pop can tell stories too?" asked Judy.

"Of course he can. What do you think, who told me stories when I was little like you?"

"And what stories does Pop have?" asked Pete. "I like the stories you tell," he said, his smile fading.

"Pop used to read me tales like Puss in Boots, Snow White or Little Red Riding Hood, you know, the classics you are also familiar with. Then one time, I told him that those stories were getting boring. That day he made up a story of his own, and we laughed a lot at that one. After that, he only told his own tales. I loved Pop's stories because they were always funny and interesting. Sometimes he even included parts of the traditional stories."

The journey was long, the kids were looking out the window. Then they asked more and more frequently: "When are we getting there?" But once every road ends, and so they arrived. Pop was very happy to see them. Pete and Judy jumped into his arms. Then, while Mum was packing, the kids ran to the garden to play and explore all the unknown things, they were playing tag and laughing. Mum and Pop were talking on the veranda. The afternoon was short, and soon it was already night time. They had dinner, then took a bath, brushed their teeth and Mum tucked them in.

"Tell us a story, Mum!"

"Pop will do it, okay?" asked Mum, turning to Pop.

He smiled at them:

"Okay, then, let the tale travel begin. Are you ready?"

"Yes, yes," shouted the kids.

"Oh, no, that's not how it works. Say it after me: to Captain Pop, I report that Traveller Pete is ready for the tale!"

"To Captain Pop, I report that Traveller Pete is ready for the tale!"

"Now you Judy."

"To Captain Pop, I report that Traveller Judy is ready for the tale!"

"Very good," smiled Pop. "And you?" he asked, turning to Mum.

"I have to report too? Well then. To Captain Pop, I report that Traveller Mum is ready for the tale" laughed Mum.

"Amazing! Then let the countdown begin. Attention please! 10, 9... now, come on, let's do it together! Come on, everybody!

"10, 9, 8, 7, 6, 5, 4, 3, 2, 1 and... 0!" they shouted together.

"And so the first story begins..."

The Giant

Woodpecker was tall and strong, a nice lad. He had broad shoulders and muscular limbs, but his face was, well, a bit brute. He had thick eyebrows and scars all over his cheeks. Let's not gloss it over: he was a particularly ugly man. He was called many names in the village. Some called him Logger, Lumberjack, or Woodborer, but he liked Woodpecker the most because he liked those birds with red feathers at the top of their heads, pecking the trees with their sharp beaks. All day long, he roamed the woods, cutting wood, twigging, rolling, doing all the work that required strength. As he was getting deeper and deeper into the forest, he didn't even realise that he was in forbidden territory. They told stories about giants living in these woods, and that they don't spare any human who steps onto their territory. Woodpecker was not afraid of anyone, especially not of the giants, as he considered himself to be one of them. Being almost 6 feet 5, he towered over the villagers.

So he was just marching forward, head down, making his way with his muscular arms and shoulders. Until, suddenly, he was lifted from the ground. First, he didn't know what was happening. He kept turning left and right until he realised he was staring directly at a giant eye the size of his own head. This eye was accompanied by a terrible, massive nose that blew air like a steam engine. A giant mouth also belonged to the eye, one so big that maybe even twenty people could fit in it, but two certainly. The eye was looking at him. The nose was sniffing him. But the mouth! The mouth was opened up and made its way to Woodpecker.

"Hey!" shouted Woodpecker. "What on earth are you doing?"

For a minute the mouth was closed, then a deep voice was heard.

"I am going to eat you."

"But why do you want to eat me? I wouldn't even be enough for dessert. Why would you waste your time with me?"

"I am eating you, because you wandered to our territory."

"Now, you see, that's it, I wandered. I didn't come here intentionally. So why don't you put me down, I go back and you go about your business."

The giant stared at the little man dumbly, trying to understand him. Then, with great difficulty, he realised what the other was trying to say.

"We can't do that."

"Why can't we? It's simple, you just bring your hand down, let your fingers out and bang! I'm out of here! Do me a favour and let's not eat each other here and just go back to where we came from."

"I have to think about it. No one has ever asked me something like this."

"But now I'm asking. So please persuade your stupid brain to bring your hand down to the ground, because I want to be on my way."

The giant opened his mouth and exhaled heavily, and Woodpecker's stomach turned as he smelled mint and mushrooms. The giant then lowered his hand slightly, giving Woodpecker some hope but not much relief.

A voice was heard in the distance. A barker was drumming and shouting, but he was too far away to understand

the words. The giant was also trying to turn towards the voice, which made the entire forest rumble.

"Stay quiet for a minute, will you?" said Woodpecker. "I can't hear anything."

The giant stiffened, he even held back his breath. This time, they heard the voice a little better:

"Whoever returns the princess the king will grant him her hand in marriage and reward him with plenty of money!"

Then he repeated the whole monologue and they learnt that the princess has blue eyes and blonde hair and she was wearing a blue skirt and a burgundy blouse when she disappeared. She is also known for wearing an emerald ring on her left hand. Anyone who has information, should contact the nearest police station.

Woodpecker furrowed his thick eyebrows and remembered that he had seen such a girl in a travelling theatre three villages away. It's about ten days' walk. If she was the princess, he was lucky.

"You giant, listen for a moment," he said to the huge head. "Let's make a deal. I know where this princess is. You could take us there rather quickly. Now put me down, or no, put me in your pocket and let's find her. Then we split the money and we're both good."

"Okay, but first I'll eat you," said the giant.

"You silly goose," Woodpecker said gently. "How are you going to find the princess if you eat me? Let's not mess with each other. Let's go get the princess! Get a hold of yourself. Come on, give me a high five."

The giant looked at him surprised. Then he gave a clumsy high five to Woodpecker, who climbed into his pocket.

"Whoa! Giddap horsey, to the left! Now to the right a little, here you go."

He said as he stretched his legs, getting comfortable in the giant's pocket.

After a short time the village appeared but the travelling theatre was gone. Woodpecker climbed down from the giant's pocket and asked everyone if they knew where the travelling theatre went. When someone was hesitant to answer he asked the giant for help and soon they knew where to go. But one young man said:

"Take me in too. The princess is held captive until she works off her debt to the theatre as it is rather unprofitable lately."

"Hop on then!" said Woodpecker.

And so they were on their way to find the travelling theatre. It only took an hour to find it.

"I will go in," said the young man. "You two stay outside."

It so happened that the theatre was rehearsing a romantic play, but the actor playing the protagonist fell ill. That's when the handsome lad stepped in and he was immediately hired for three months. The young man looked at the princess and fell so in love with her that his hands and feet trembled. He drew her to him, and according to the play, she had to embrace him. That was when he saw the thick chain on her ankle. A burly guard stood next to the stage, making sure that the chain stayed on the girl's ankle.

"Be not afraid, my dear!" said the young man and sneaked out of the theatre to find Woodpecker and the giant who were resting by the brook.

He told them what he saw inside. That was all Woodpecker needed. He sent the young man back on the stage, who wasn't only handsome anymore but also very much in love. When the play began, the giant picked up the stage, and the guard in charge of the princess fell off. Then the giant took the stage with the princess and the young man straight to the palace. There he put down the stage and they finished the play, then handed the princess over to the king.

Everyone was overjoyed in the palace. They took off the chain from the princess' ankle. Then the king turned to Woodpecker:

"My dear son, since you brought back my daughter you'll have the reward: her hand and plenty of money."

"Wait a moment, my dear king. As you can see there are three of us. Let this handsome young man have your daughter's hand in marriage, as he is already in love with her. Then the giant and I will split the money."

And so they did it that way. They had a big wedding, the newlyweds were happy. When Woodpecker got the money he even gave some to the couple. Then said to the giant:

"Now you silly goose. Here is the money, now we can have a nice feast."

"Okay, but first I'll eat you," said the giant.

"But why would you eat me?"

"Because you stepped on our territory and we eat everyone who does. We can't let them know we actually exist."

"Listen, you idiot," said Woodpecker. "If you haven't noticed everyone has seen you. So let's skip eating me and celebrate like good pals."

He held his hand out for a high-five. The giant smiled and gave him one. And so they started to celebrate, maybe they still do if the giant hasn't eaten Woodpecker.

"That's it?" asked the kids. "Tell it again!"

So Pop told them again. But when they asked for it once more he only laughed.

"Oh, no, that's not how it works. I only repeat the stories once. Tomorrow, if you want to hear it, I will tell another tale."

"We want to," they said in unison.

"But what will it be about, Pop? Will you tell us? Please, please!" said Judy.

"As the saying goes: curious minds find little sleep."

"There's no such saying," laughed Mum.

She tucked in the kids and kissed them goodnight, then she and Pop left the room. Pete and Judy probably weren't that curious as they fell asleep quickly. Or maybe they just had a long day, who knows.

Day Two

The next morning, when Pete and Judy arrived in the kitchen for breakfast, the freshly baked pancakes and maple syrup were already on the table. They ate so much that Mum couldn't believe it.

"Wow, you two sure have an appetite. Did some leprechaun switch you out in your sleep?"

"They should have a good appetite," said Pop.

"Will you tell us a tale, Pop?" asked the kids, not even paying attention to Mum's question.

"In the evening I will. The story always comes after bath time."

That day they went to the lake, swam and ran around on the coast, played ball. They studied the tadpoles along the shore. When the water got warmer, they dove in. Pop went with them, of course, so they remained in safe distance from the shore. They splashed each other, and then, when Mum came in she also got some water. Pop chased the kids and then took turns throwing them up in the air. They screamed when they fell into the water and begged him to throw them again, as far as possible. Mum was very happy because she was a bit worried that the kids wouldn't like it at Pop's. Though they saw each other often, they had never slept over. She was glad that they were having such a good time together. She wondered if it was due to the storytelling last night. Pop had worked a miracle, as he had done with her back when she was a kid. She wiped her eyes, moved by the events. That's how it is: when we are the happiest, that's when we look the saddest.

The morning went by quickly, and the kids ate a lot for lunch before continuing to play, giggling and screaming. Mum and Pop were watching them from the shade, talking about a bit of everything. Later they ate watermelon. And Mum was once again surprised because she thought the kids didn't like watermelon.

Pete and Judy spent a lot of time playing in the garden before going inside to watch television. They were grabbing the remote from each other's hands, switching the channels, but they couldn't find a movie they liked. So they threw the remote on the bed and started playing tag instead. Finally, the evening arrived, and they were getting more and more excited. They bathed faster than they had ever before. After brushing their teeth and drying their hair, they dashed into their room. Very soon they were in bed demanding a story in unison.

"We want the tale! We want the tale!"

"Are you ready?"

"To Captain Pop, I report that Traveller Pete is ready for the tale!" rushed out Pete.

"To Captain Pop, I report that Traveller Judy is ready for the tale!" laughed Judy.

"To Captain Pop, I report that Traveller Mum is ready for the tale!" said Mum too.

They were all buzzing to hear Pop's new story.

"Amazing! Then let the countdown begin. Attention please! 10, 9... now, come one, let's do it together! Come on, everybody!

"10, 9, 8, 7, 6, 5, 4, 3, 2, 1 and... 0!" they shouted in unison.

"And so the second story begins..."

Remote

"Bring butter and ham, and tissues..." listed Amelia the things she wanted but Todd was already out the door.

He was short but muscular, always running quickly to meet her wife's demands. The others were just laughing at him: "Here comes Todd, never remembers what he is told." But Todd didn't pay attention, he just ran past them, fast like lightning, one of his feet already almost at home.

When he finally arrived, Amelia was already complaining: "Why didn't you bring soap? I've been running my mouth for nothing? You have the memory of a goldfish."

Todd simply looked down, ran, packed, cooked, and did whatever she asked. Nonetheless, Amelia always found a reason to argue with him. Then one morning, as he was just waking up, Amelia was already yelling at him.

"You are still sleeping? Where is my coffee and..." he didn't hear the rest.

He put on his slippers and ran straight to the kitchen. As he brought in the freshly made coffee Amelia was smiling. Todd was afraid in advance, because when Amelia smiled it meant no good.

"Do you know, what day is it today, Todd?"

"No," he said, with his tail between his legs.

"Today is my birthday!" cried Amelia. "And you didn't bring me a cake! You good-for-nothing! Now go and bring me a cake made from fresh strawberries," said Amelia.

Her face was twisted by anger, but inside she was laughing. She knew that there were no fresh strawberries at this time of year, February. She also knew she could scold his husband again if he returned home without a strawberry cake. Because nagging and grumbling made her really happy.

Todd quickly dressed up. He put on his coat and wool scarf and walked outside into the howling wind. He ran as fast as he could, trying to warm himself up by rubbing his arms with his gloved hands.

"Here comes henpecked Todd!" the people said, laughing. "Such a manly man! His wife would beat him if he did not do as she asked. He is such a disgrace."

But Todd had worse things to worry about then listening to them. He kept wondering where he could get strawberries, and fresh ones at that, baked into a cake. The snowdrops weren't even blooming, let alone the strawberries. He was running, his muscular legs flexing, taking him into the forest.

"Amelia! Amelia, why are you doing this to me?" he cried.

Shivering from the cold he sat down on a bough, maybe he even dozed off. Then somehow, with great effort, he opened his eyes, because he smelt smoke. Someone made a small campfire nearby. Todd, his legs nearly frozen, made his way to the fire, where an elderly man was warming his hands. He was throwing twigs into the flames.

"What's up Henpecked Todd? Had enough of the good stuff?" he asked then laughed like a hyena. "Come here and warm your hands. You'll never find strawberries at this time of the year, you coward."

Todd joined him, he didn't argue, he was used to being mocked. But he still asked:

"How do you know that I'm looking for strawberries?"

"Come one! Everybody knows. Amelia is shouting so loud, the whole village hears it. Well, maybe not the whole village, but a lot of people," a pause. "Okay, so not that many people, but I know and that's what matters. Now

what do you want to do? You can't even buy that in Aldi or Lidl, not even in Tesco."

"I don't know," said Todd. "But I can't go home without strawberries."

"Are you sure?" asked the man.

Then without turning to him said:

"Now, can you see that box over there, Todd?"

Todd looked around and saw a cake box.

"Now, there happens to be a strawberry cake in it. If you want it, I will give it to you. You'll also get a remote with it."

"A remote? Why would I need a remote for a cake? That's only good for a television, isn't it?"

"Not for the cake, you idiot! Not even for a television," said the man. "It's for Amelia," when he saw Todd's puzzled expression he explained it: "If you press one of the buttons on the remote while thinking about something, it will happen. Just think about it, press any of the buttons and it will happen."

Todd's eyes widened. He started to realise that this could mean that he will finally have some freedom. He ran to the box. And indeed it smelled like mouth-watering strawberries. And on the top of it there was the remote.

"Are you sure it's working?" he asked.

"Of course," snapped the man. "Made in Japan! It's not some fake," when he saw the mischievous smile on Todd's face he added: "But never press the return button. Be careful with that one! Now run home to Amelia, but don't mess things up."

He slapped Todd on the back. And for an old man he was in good strength because Todd fell face first into the snow. By the time he got up the man was nowhere to be seen.

Todd brushed off his clothes and ran home. He was worried that Amelia will have a quarrel again. He wasn't surprised. Amelia started shouting the moment he stepped inside the house.

"Where were you? You tramp!"

"I brought a cake..." he wanted to say, but Amelia kept on insulting him.

That's when he remembered the remote and pressed one of the buttons, thinking: "I'm so happy that you are finally home!"

And lo and behold Amelia suddenly said:

"I'm so happy that you are finally home! You are the best husband. I love you so much my dear Todd. Come and give a kiss to you sweet Amelia," and she was saying kinder and sweeter things each time.

Her eyes were wide in horror, she couldn't understand why she was saying these thing when she wanted to scold her husband.

"You are the sweetest husband in the whole world," she said, then immediately covered her mouth.

Todd was getting the hang of using the remote. He smiled on the things Amelia said. Then snickered, in the end he laughed so hard he started crying.

"Oh, my dear Todd, I will do the washing after we ate the cake."

Todd couldn't take it anymore. He laid down on the bed holding his stomach from laughing so hard. He dropped the remote and it fell on the ground. Amelia didn't need anymore, she picked it up with a triumphant look. And just as she saw Todd doing it, she said what she had been keeping to herself.

"I will give you a lesson now, Todd. Go jump in a lake!" and she pressed the return button.

But then, like a fast-motion shot, he ran out of the house, through the village, picking her feet backwards and disappearing faster and faster in the distance.

Todd just watched her then realised which button she pressed. He was laughing for a long time after that. Then he got up, cleaned out the house, put everything back to its place. As time passed he entered several half-marathons and won all of them. Thanks to all the running he had to do next to Amelia he had strong legs. Even the villagers looked up to him, they no longer called him henpecked. By time he met a sweet young girl and they lived happily ever after together. He took the batteries out of the remote and put it in a box in the attic, just as the instructions said.

And Amelia? Well, she jumped in a lake. But even at the bottom of it she kept talking and talking. The fish tolerated it for a while, but then they grew legs and walked away rather than listening to her all day. So she is still at the bottom of the lake, all alone, if the lake hasn't dried out yet.

The kids giggled for a few minutes after the story ended, then they kept on repeating: the fish grew legs and walked away. And they laughed at it like it was the best joke they had ever heard. Of course, they begged Pop to repeat the story. And, of course Pop did, just like the night before.

"And what happened to Amelia? Did she go home in the end?" asked Judy.

"No, she didn't," said Mum, it was in the story after all.

"It is better this way. I don't want her to go home," said Pete.

"Now, it's time to sleep tale travellers," smiled Mum.

"Traveller Pete is almost asleep."

"Pop, what story will you tell tomorrow?" asked Judy.

"You will find out tomorrow," said Pop, stroking her hair.

"But I don't want to wait until tomorrow."

"Then go to sleep fast and it will be tale time in no time."

Their eyes were already closed and soon enough they were both snoring.

"Thanks Dad," said Mum.

"What are you thanking me for?"

"The stories. It's like I'm a kid again. And these are even better tales than the ones you told back in the day."

"I don't think. You simply grew up and understand them more."

"Maybe," said Mum, she also fell asleep fast that night.

Day Three

When the kids smelled the freshly cooked bacon, fried egg, sausage, and hash browns, they rushed down to the kitchen, their stomachs growling. Mum told Pop that they would not eat all of that because they had already eaten so much yesterday. However, she was once again surprised.

"What was in those eggs?" she asked. "I can't believe how much they ate again. You must have put something in the food, Dad.

"Where are we going today, Pop?" asked Judy.

"Today we are going bird watching. There's a lookout not far away. We'll bring binoculars to study the birds. We'll see storks and all kinds of songbirds, and mallards. Who knows, maybe even a fox will wander by."

"A fox?" cheered Pete. "Let's get going then!"

And so they did. They put on baseball caps to protect their heads from the sun and applied sunscreen to their arms and legs. They put the binoculars in the backpack. After approximately thirty minutes of walking, they arrived at the lookout. Pop said something about all the plants they passed. They saw frogs, water snakes, all kinds of fish and lizards. Suddenly, a stork flew over the reeds. The kids were cheering and taking the binoculars from each other's hands. They could not stop turning their heads because there was so much to see. After some time, they noticed a fox in the distance, but it refused to come closer, so they only examined it through binoculars. However, the best part was when the mallards got so close to the lookout that they could almost touch them. On their way home, they spent some time studying the frogs and tadpoles.

When they arrived at the house, they were telling Mum everything they had seen. They liked all of them. Judy gushed about the water snakes, while Pete talked about the fox in the distance. Mum's smile got bigger and bigger. She never imagined the holiday would be so good.

They had fish and chips for lunch. Mum almost opened her mouth to say that they would definitely not eat all the food, but before she could say anything, they were already eating with gusto. So she did not say anything and just looked at them happily. They hadn't even swallowed the last bites when they were already in the garden.

Then the evening came again, and the kids bathed in military discipline, like two little soldiers. They didn't spend much time in the bathtub. They brushed their teeth and tucked each other in so Pop could begin the story as soon as possible. They didn't even need to be warned about the reporting.

"Traveller Judy is ready for the tale."

"Traveller Pete is ready for the tale."

"Traveller Mum is ready for the tale."

Pop saluted to the tale troopers and they started the countdown.

"10, 9, 8, 7, 6, 5, 4, 3, 2, 1, and... 0!" they shouted in unison.

"So let the third story begin..."

The Seven-Headed Dragon

❝ My dear king, shouldn't we impose a new tax on the people?" asked the Councillor. "The treasury is short of income."

"No, I don't want a rebellion," said the King.

"Only if they don't want to pay the tax."

"Don't be a fool. Why would they want to pay another tax?"

"Your majesty, give me some time."

And so the Councillor sent men in disguise. They incited the public by claiming that the rich use far more water than they do, which is unfair. They should put a tax on water. Everyone was taxed, but they installed metres to keep track of how much water they used. They happened to be made and installed by the Councillor's company, which was also in charge of the repairing. And somehow the metres broke down every month and everyone had to pay for the repair themselves. The Councillor's land had a stream with abundant water, but the law prohibited taxing natural waters. As a result, the Councillor didn't need to pay, not even a penny.

However, he didn't stop there. He convinced the king that people shouldn't breathe the majestic air of his country for free, and tax on the air was also imposed. The Councillor created a clever machine that measured air intake, and they were required to pay accordingly. Poor people talked less and less because they used more

air when speaking. They could only take off the machines when they were in the tavern. However, even there, if they did not drink any of the Councillor's drinks, they had to pay because they were using shared air. The people were getting increasingly desperate. By the end of the month, they had returned all of their earnings to the King, or a large portion of them to the Councillor.

The Councillor covered his property with a huge bell jar. He claimed that he did not have to pay the tax because he was producing his own air. He spent the entire day walking between the beautiful flowers in his garden, considering what new tax he should levy on the people. But in the end, he rejected all of his ideas because he feared there would be no one left to pay taxes. With a long groan, he put his thoughts on hold and fell asleep.

The King lived happily in his palace, unaware of his people's misery. He watched his daughter lovingly, as she grew, almost unnoticed, into a beautiful woman. She had golden blond hair and blue eyes, and when she laughed, even the birds fell silent in envy.

Then, one day, a student was travelling through the country. He was taken aback when they placed the masked machine on his head and counted each breath he took. He was even more shocked to learn that he had to pay tax on every sip of water and every litre of bathing water. When he asked the people on the street: "How can you live like this?" They did not really respond to him, just walked away with their heads down.

"But is not there someone who would speak up about this?" he exclaimed.

"Don't shout, the King's men will come and take you," they whispered.

"Fine," said the student. "I won't participate in this ridicule."

And he was already on his way out of the kingdom, but seeing the poor people gave him an idea.

"What is closest to the king's heart?" Something taken from him would cause him great pain."

"His daughter," said the people. "She is very precious to him. But he will never lose her because she is so well guarded that no harm can come to her."

The student went away to think about what he should do. He fell asleep while thinking and awoke to a very wet, very large, and very disgusting tongue licking his face.

"Hey! Stop this in an instant," he said.

That is when he realised a huge dragon was licking him.

"What on earth were you thinking?" he asked. "I am lucky you didn't eat me or breathe fire in my face."

The dragon was looking at him shocked.

"Don't you know we are vegan? And none of us breathes fire either."

"And where are all your other heads?"

"What are you talking about? Are you drunk? Do you have more heads than one? Have you ever been to a Biology class?"

"Well, a professor at the university always talks about how he rode a seven-headed dragon once when he was younger. Others also talked about many-headed dragons. You know, like Hydras? And there are all those motifs on shields and stuff."

"Oh, that's only an urban legend. My great-grandfather made it up, so people would leave us alone. Like when Big Foot spread the rumour about the Yeti, so people would look for him at Everest instead."

The student was a bit confused. However, as he was looking at the dragon measuring and examining him he came up with an idea. Well, sort of.

"Let me ask you. Do you happen to have a larger relative? Don't get me wrong, but you are quite small for a dragon.

"Well, I have a brother, he goes to the gym quite often. You should see his biceps!" said the dragon. "He's a handsome lad or dragon."

"Well then, take me to him," said the student.

And they were on their way to find the brother dragon.

He was much bigger than his younger brother, but the student was still dissatisfied. He said a seven-headed dragon would be more convincing. Brother Dragon tried to explain to him that he simply could not grow six more heads. Not even Schwarzenegger had a workout plan for that. The student then described his plan, which involved kidnapping the King's daughter to get her hand in marriage and half of the kingdom. How it is typically done, and then he can save the people.

"You still believe in fairy tales?" asked the dragonboy.

The student hummed and mumbled before snapping his fingers and disappearing. He took some photos of the dragon and placed large screens around his head to make it appear that he had multiple heads.

"How does it look?" asked the student.

"Want me to be honest?"

"Please don't," he said, disappointed. "They always say OLED screens look good even in sunlight."

"And you believe those ads?" asked the dragon

Then suddenly his face lit up and he dashed away.

"Hey, where are you going?" he shouted after him, like Han Solo to Chewbacca.

"I'll be back," he said.

And soon he indeed came back, accompanied by six giant snakes. He approached the student and placed his hand on his shoulder, reassuring him.

"We have signed a contract. They will act like the six heads, and you will reward them handsomely," said the dragon.

"And if it doesn't work?" asked the student, frightened.

"Then they will eat you. But do not worry, they are pretty good actors," he reassured him, but without much success.

They climbed on Dragon Brother's shoulders and turned their heads in different directions.

"What does it look like? Like I have seven heads, right?"

"Not really," replied the student, already envisioning the snakes suffocating and devouring him.

"Wait a minute!" said the younger dragon.

He got a snake skin from somewhere and put it on his brother's head, covering the snakes' bodies. It appeared that they all belonged to the same body.

"This looks better," said the student but he still wasn't convinced that he made a good decision getting himself into this mess.

"Don't you worry," said the Dragon Brother. "Don't forget about the power of surprise. These people have never seen a seven-headed dragon, not even a one-headed one."

The student accepted the unchangeable and they set off to the kingdom. He himself hid behind the neck of one of the snakes to direct the action. When they reached the gate, the dragon charged, broke it down and did not stop until he reached the courtyard, where the princess was playing in the sun. The dragon caught the girl, and he waiting for the student to give him instructions, but he could have waited for a long time. The student, seeing the princess, was so awestruck that he could neither see nor hear anything but her beauty. Fortunately, the mission had been rehearsed earlier, the assistants knew what to do. Leaving the surprised and horrified people and royal

guard behind, the dragon ran off back to their home. There he dumped the girl and the student and let him explain himself. But the student only blushed, and sweated, and stuttered, and his eyes bulged. Well, it wasn't an attractive sight, that's for sure. The princess just grumbled, how could he think of such a thing, and besides, she's the princess, and what was he thinking, and she wouldn't shut up. And the student thought that no one had ever quarrelled with him so beautifully. Then he forced himself to shout at her to shut her up.

"Look, princess. We did not kidnap you to harm you, but because this is the only way your father will restore the people's freedom, which was taken by your uncle, the Councillor."

Then he told her about the Councillor's wicked methods for taxing the people, which made them more and more miserable and poor. The princess listened to him and noticed how reasonable and convincing he was. Then she also realised he was right. Then she noticed his handsome face and soothing voice. As they walked to the brook, their hands occasionally touched, and the princess blushed. Her breathing quickened. She soon wished to stay here with this nice lad instead of returning to the palace.

When the dragon abducted his daughter, the King was furious. No one could talk to him. Then, as time passed and he received no news about his daughter, he remembered that, according to legend, dragons eat young unmarried girls, which increased his concern. Furthermore, the dragon was rather ugly; his heads resembled snakes. He promised that whoever found his daughter would receive half of his kingdom, as well as his daughter's hand in marriage. The barkers spread the King's words, and it eventually reached the student.

Maybe the snakes will not eat me after all, he thought, because the reptiles had been circling him for some time as no news had come from the palace. Now, the student mounted the dragon and set out with the princess for the palace. As soon as they arrived, the guards got scared and left the gate open, allowing the student to ride the dragon all the way to the king. There they stopped, and he said:

"My dearest king, the moment I heard you were looking for your daughter, I set out to find her. I slashed the dragon's six heads until only one remained, and I could ride him here with you, daughter. Now I hand her over to her father," he said, helping her get off the saddle.

Everyone in the palace was overjoyed. The princess ran to her father and jumped into his arms, tears of joy on her face. The student then took the king aside and told him about what his brother, the Councillor, had done to the people. The King's eyes widened; he did not want to believe it, but then the student showed him the Councillor's estate, which had a net on it, holes in it that let all the air through, and the air-maker was nothing more than a shabby little hairdryer. The King was furious and banished the Councillor. After that, he went to the Pension Office, where he learned that the correspondence course he completed at the King Training Academy also counted towards his years of service. So he happily retired, leaving the kingdom and his daughter to the student. The student, as promised, gave plenty to the snakes and repealed all of the Councillor's taxes, leaving only the old ones. The people worked happily and the kingdom prospered. For there were only as many taxes as they could pay for. Just like in the fairy tales.

"But Pop I would be scared if I saw six snakes," said Pete.

"Why would you? They didn't eat anybody."

"Yes, but they are still scary."

"These snakes are harmless," Pop assured them. "And this is not even the most important aspect of the story. What matters is that the student outsmarted everyone."

"Yes! He was a great student," said Judy. "I was rooting for him. I am happy he married the princess in the end. I want a student like him to be my husband."

"Well, you need to sleep a bit more for that," laughed Mum.

"And I will be as clever as the student!" said Pete proudly.

They said goodnight to the kids, and Pete and Judy fell asleep fast, there was no need for lullabies. So many things happened that day that they were driven to sleep by them.

"Dad, you are making these stories up on the spot?" asked Mum.

"Yes, but it makes me so happy, storytelling. It even makes me younger, believe me."

Mum had trouble falling asleep that night. He was thinking about the stories and how much fun the kids had here. Then she remembered when she was a little girl, watching the ducks, now she felt like a kid again. Then fatigue proved to be stronger than stories, she fell asleep too. In her dreams, she visited the seven-headed dragon and occasionally smiled in her sleep.

Day Four

The kids awoke to the smell of freshly made toast. They dashed to the kitchen as if they had not eaten in months. Pop spread baked beans on the toast, and they drank warm tea with it. Mum was surprised again as she looked back and forth between the children. What happened to them? Some miracle? They were eating with a good appetite, dishes they would not have eaten before, no matter how much their parents begged. Pop had some secrets, that's for sure.

"Where are we going today?" asked Pete, mouth full of beans.

"Today? We are going on a hike," said Pop.

"On a hike?" asked Judy, excited.

"Yes, we are going to visit the Dragon Spring," he said.

Then he explained that there is not always water in the brook, only when the dragon is awake. You can even hear his voice at those times.

Of course, the kids loved the legend. They were on their way in no time. However, the spring was barely trickling. They didn't hear the sound of any dragon, though the kids even put their ears to the rock. They were all disappointed, but they continued their walk and went to the nearby lake. Reeds were growing near the shore, so Pop cut some mace for them, which the kids loved so much that they were clenching them even on the train ride home. They all screamed as they entered the tunnel, including Mum. They were laughing so hard that Mum teared up. At the terminus, they got off and walked around, while the kids played tag in the meadow.

They decided to eat homemade beef burgers for lunch at a nearby restaurant. Pete and Judy were amazed when they saw the open kitchen and how the hamburgers were made. The burgers were huge, so Pop was surprised that even the kids ate the entire thing. He was even more surprised when they ate all the pancakes he and Mum made for dinner.

Then the evening arrived. All the tale travellers reported to the captain.

"Traveller Judy is ready for the tale."

"Traveller Pete is ready for the tale."

"Traveller Mum is ready for the tale."

Then the usual countdown started.

"10, 9, 8, 7, 6, 5, 4, 3, 2, 1, and... 0!" they shouted in unison.

"So let the fourth story begin..."

Jousting tournament

Gustav Joachim Wolfgang Amadeus Wallenberg began shouting. Rather miserably at that. The reason was that he stumbled upon his armour while entering his room, and he held his sword so awkwardly that it became entangled in the armour around his knee, preventing him from standing up. Gustav Joachim Wolfgang Amadeus Wallenberg, King Ulrich II's thirteenth knight was lying on the ground trying to get out the sword from his armour. He was trying so hard that he teared up; this seemed like a good enough reason to cry out for help. He shouted once, then twice. By the time help arrived, he had managed to remove the sword from his armour. The patissier entered, carrying a Yorkshire pudding that he was about to deliver to him.

"I will help, sir," he said.

He then managed to drop the pudding on top of the knight.

"Oh, for crying out loud!" The knight looked up to the sky before snapping at the patissier. "Do you have more puddings? Or will you help me get up?"

"Of course," said the patissier, helping him stand up.

He was surprised to discover that, despite his armour, the knight was not particularly heavy.

"Then help me get rid of this hideous armour as well!"

As the armour fell to the ground and they removed the helmet, the patissier noticed what was wearing underneath. He was covered in sponge, had shoulder pads, and was wearing high heels to make him appear taller. Finally, there stood the thirteenth knight, dressed in a tank top and trousers, no taller than 5 feet 1 and weighing 105 pounds. The patissier was stunned, unable to believe what he was seeing.

"Why are you looking at me?" asked the knight.

He went to the mirror and flexed his arms, but he was so thin that only the skin moved. He had no muscle on his body. The knight sat down, jaded by the sight, and looked down at the ground with a deep sigh.

"I assume you are surprised. How can someone like this be a knight, right?"

"Of course not," he assured him. "Well, okay, I do. You look rather small for a knight."

"That's my problem," said the knight.

He licked his fingers after wiping some pudding off his neck. It was delicious.

"What can I do with a body like that? The jousting tournament is next week. Whoever wins receives half of the kingdom and his daughter's hand in marriage. And whoever loses the duel is eliminated from the tournament. Guess who I am up against? Who could it be? Of course, the Black Knight, the best duellist! 6 feet 6 and 260 pounds, his arms are larger than my thighs!"

"Well, that is not difficult to accomplish," said the patissier. "What are you going to do?"

"Nothing, I'm thinking about fleeing. They have already placed a bet that if I win, they will pay sixteen times the prize money. Nobody will bet on the Black Knight because it is so obvious that he will win.

"Multiplied by sixteen?" The patissier's eyes widened. "That'd be worth winning."

"Winning? Are you crazy? Have you seen that man? I am only alive because he cannot see to the sides and cannot see me. Don't waste your money by betting on me."

However, the patissier was adamant. He was walking up and down, saying words like "crush," "knock," and "yrotciv". The knight could not quite understand the last word, but it must have been an important one because he repeated it several times.

"noitulos eht evah I!"

"Excuse me?"

"noitulos eht evah I!"

"Could you try it backwards?"

"I have the solution!" said the patissier.

His name, by the way, was Guiseppe.

"And would you like to share it, maybe?"

"I will make you a sword to fight with."

"I am hoping it will be lighter than the one I have now. I can't even lift this one, let alone hold it."

"If you would allow me to finish... So this one will be made of sugar and coated in honey. When the Black Knight approaches, simply hold it slightly tilted in front of you. He will cut through the sword, and as he does, the honey will drip onto his hand, then onto his trousers, down to the saddle, and eventually, he will fall off the horse."

"You are crazy!"

"For sure, but that's not the point."

"And if it won't drip on the saddle, then what?"

"Nothing extra, he will cut off your head, I guess."

"Nothing extra? Listen to me! It is my head after all, and I got quite used to having it. I would like to keep it."

"Well, yes," chewed Guiseppe. "If you really want, I can give you a dagger with raspberry syrup in it. When he cuts your sword, you stab his saddle, the syrup pours out, and voilà! I receive a thousand and six hundred golds."

"You only think about winning," chugged the knight.

"Yes, but don't bother with that. If I win you will be still alive. We will have a rehearsal tomorrow," he said as he walked out the door.

The knight stood before the mirror and tried to flex his non-existent muscles once more, then gave up with a sigh. He realised that his fate lay in the hands of the patissier. After devouring the last morsels of the Yorkshire pudding, he let out a hiccup and fell into a deep sleep.

As the sun began to rise, Guiseppe emerged with a dagger and a sword. After mounting his horse, he instructed the knight to do the same. Then, as they had planned, Guiseppe held his sword in position. The knight made a stride forward then he sliced the sugar sword and plunged the dagger into the saddle. The honey oozed from the sword at a sluggish pace, eventually dripping onto Guiseppe's hand, causing him to lose his grip on the sword. Miraculously, he managed to stay in the saddle, but as he did, the raspberry syrup from the dagger splattered beside his thigh, causing him to slide slowly off the horse.

"Was this convincing to you?" asked Gustav Joachim Wolfgang Amadeus Wallenberg the thirteenth knight.

"To be honest, not really. This needs a bit more planning."

"What do you want to plan? Tomorrow is the tournament, and this time I will be laying on the ground, sliced in half. And you are still planning?" The knight snapped at him, his voice becoming thin.

"Okay, then I will put syrup in the sword too. And I will talk to my beekeeper friend about opening the hives right before the tournament so the bees will be hungry. Trust me!"

The knight glanced at the patissier before heading off to pray, feeling disheartened by the seemingly hopeless plan.

The next day, Guiseppe asked his boss to lend him a hundred golds and bet on the knight's victory. "Are you stupid! You have this much money?" When he took the receipt, he received such sayings. He helped the knight to get ready. He cried at first, then swore at the patissier to leave him alone with this ridiculous plan, but Guiseppe refused to back down. He dragged the knight to the arena, put him on the horse, and handed him the sword and dagger. He himself ran to the beekeeper. When he saw Gustav Joachim Wolfgang Amadeus Wallenberg, King Ulrich II's thirteenth knight, the Black Knight laughed so hard that he coughed and teared up. The king then opened the duel. The Black Knight's vision was slightly blurry, but he did not take the duel too seriously. He cut slowly towards the thirteenth knight, which proved to be a good decision because the raspberry syrup had more time to flow from the sword. Surprised by the fluid, the Black Knight dropped his sword, and as the syrup from the dagger flew into his lap, he began to wobble in the saddle. However, he was the Black Knight after all, and he was able to maintain his balance. The crowd went wild as they cheered for the mighty champion. But they did not count on the bees, who attacked and stung his thighs furiously. The knight needed nothing more; he opened his legs to escape the bees and fell off the horse in an instant. Gustav Joachim Wolfgang Amadeus Wallenberg was stunned when he realised he had won the duel.

The princess' cheeks were on fire as she fled the stands. There was no way she was going to marry such a coward. As she was furiously punching the air, she noticed a young, handsome man arguing in front of the betting office because they refused to pay him.

"I did win! The knight knocked the Black Knight out of the saddle."

"He didn't knock out anybody. It was a fraud! The Black Knight fell because of the bees," argued the officer.

The princess went to see what was going on because she believed the man was correct, and he was also familiar to her. After more shouting, Guiseppe finally got his money. She only noticed the princess after that.

"Now look at me," said the princess. "You seem suspicious. How is it possible that you were the only one in the kingdom to bet on this coward?"

"I am just a lucky guy, I guess," he stuttered, blushing as he was captivated by the princess' beauty.

"Say that to the jury," said the princess.

And she kept questioning him until the patissier explained how he won. The princess chuckled, then gazed into his eyes for a bit longer than appropriate. She grew quite fond of the clever man. Then she said goodbye and went to see his father.

"My dear father," she said sweetly. "I'm sure there's no doubt that the knight didn't actually defeat the Black Knight. He only fell off his saddle because of the bees. You should arrange a rematch."

It did not take much time to persuade the king. He was not happy that the mini knight, as the others called him, would get his daughter's hand and everything else. He announced that, due to the unfortunate circumstances, there will be a rematch in which the thirteenth knight can prove himself worthy of the throne.

When Gustav Joachim Wolfgang Amadeus Wallenberg learned the news, he immediately began packing. He packed two sets of clothes and enough food for three days in his bag and purchased a one-way plane ticket to Australia. He had no intentions of returning. However, just as he finished, the patissier entered his room. He was furious. Firstly, because they took his money. Secondly, he was in love. And thirdly, he wanted to beat the knight.

"You are not going anywhere," he said, dragging the knight back from the doorstep. "I have a different idea. You will duel with the Black Knight or I will be the one cutting off your head."

The knight considered his options. The plane ticket seemed to be the better option, but it was now out of reach.

"Okay, what is your plan?" he asked.

The patissier told him that this time he would bring a real sword, but there would be itching powder in his left hand. When the Black Knight hits his sword, he should hold it lightly. This will be unexpected, and the Black Knight will lean forward in his saddle. That is when he should throw all of the itching powder at him, under the armour.

The knight had heard enough. He dashed to the window to jump out, but it was closed. He wanted to climb beneath the bed, but the patissier was faster and lifted it. There was nothing else to do, so he accepted that he would carry his head home in his hands.

The morning arrived, and the patissier returned to the betting office. This time, he bet one hundred and sixty times the winning amount on the knight. They threatened to beat him if he cheated again, but he paid little attention. The Black Knight was furious, he threw himself at Gustav Joachim Wolfgang Amadeus Wallenberg, who didn't have to hold the sword lightly to drop it in an instant. The Black Knight lost his balance, and Gustav threw the itching powder at him. It was a small movement that the people on the stands missed, but the king in the VIP section saw it clearly.

The Black Knight's skin became so itchy that he shouted and let go of the reins to scratch himself. He lost his balance and fell from the saddle. The people only saw that he fell after he hit the small knight. He was squirming on the ground and crying because he could not get his hands under his armour. They took him away on a stretcher, and once outside of the arena, he removed his clothes and scratched himself bloody.

The king asked for the knight, smiled at him, and said quietly:

"Now, were you the one who came up with this idea? You can tell me the truth."

Fearing that he would be punished, the knight called for the patissier. Guiseppe looked at the king with some unease, then at the princess with affection.

"He was the one who came up with the idea, my king. Please, forgive us for the fraud, but this was the only way to defeat the knight."

The king chuckled. He looked at the knight, then at the patissier, back at the king, then at the patissier again, and finally at his daughter, who was still staring at the patissier. The king finally understood everything because he was not only a king, but also elderly and wise. He said:

"Well, if the trick was what defeated the knight, the patissier should receive the prize because he devised the plan. I assume he was also the one who made the sword for the first duel. This means that he will have my daughter's hand in marriage and half the kingdom. "And maybe my daughter agrees as well," he said, smiling. "But you, Gustav Joachim Wolfgang Amadeus Wallenberg, will now serve as King Guiseppe I's knight. And I wish you a good life for your bravery in the duel."

The patissier vowed to be a good king. He did not ask for his bet money, and some sources say he made a wise decision because the betting officer really wanted to beat him.

When Pop told the knight's story again – as every tale had to be told twice –they laughed just as hard as the first time. Pop was very happy that they loved the stories so much.

"Pop, is this itching powder a real thing?"

"Of course it is. And did you know that many theatrical props are made from sugar?"

"But what props?"

"Take mirrors, for example. If they were made of real glass and broke on stage, they would cause a lot of damage."

"But they can't make such a sword, right?"

"I don't know," said Pop. "I am not a blacksmith or a patissier, but perhaps they can make something like that.

What I do know is that all tale travellers should go to sleep now."

"Pop, do you know what tomorrow's story will be?" asked Judy.

"I have no idea, but you will find out tomorrow evening for sure."

"Could it be about a puppy?"

"I am not sure what it will be about, but you should really sleep or I will bring the itching powder."

The kids fell asleep giggling, Mum had a hard time tucking them in as they were afraid that they might get itching powder on them.

Mum talked a bit more with Pop. She loved it here; the programmes, the dining, the stories—everything was better than she expected. She fell asleep with a big smile.

Day Five

Next morning Pete and Judy woke to the smell of breakfast. Mum and Pop made fried bread. They ran down on the stars so fast that they almost fell over. They ate one slice after another. Both their hands and his lips were covered in oil. They ate so much that they were panting in their seats, but they still cut a slice in half.

"Dad, did I eat this much as a kid?" Mum asked. "Because I can't remember."

"No, you didn't eat this much. But it is summer, and we have a lot of programmes; they need the energy."

"Okay. It is just that every day I wonder if I am doing something wrong or you are doing something right, because they are eating more than ever before."

"It's because of the fresh air and the variety of programmes. Come on, eat one more slice."

"Thanks Dad, but I'm full."

Pop has already made plans. He took them boating. Everyone put on life jackets and they got into the massive canoe. They navigated through the reeds; Mum and Pop took the lead, but the kids also had paddles to help them. When it got hot Pop moored the boat. They found a spot in the shade and settled down to fish. The kids were happy to help Pop and they were thrilled each time he caught a fish. Later, Pete and Judy tried fishing as well. Pete caught a smaller fish, but Pop threw it back because it was too small and would grow much larger. They caught a few more fish and saved them for lunch.

They made fish soup, the kids were buzzing to eat as soon as they smelled it. The soup was spicy, but they ate it up and even asked for a refill. They got back in the canoe and shouted when a fish jumped from the water. In the afternoon, they played in the garden while Mum and Pop prepared dinner.

The day came to an end, as they all do. After their bath, they jumped into bed and waited impatiently for the story. They all reported:

"Traveller Judy is ready for the tale."

"Traveller Pete is ready for the tale."

"Traveller Mum is ready for the tale."

Then the ceremonious countdown started.

"10, 9, 8, 7, 6, 5, 4, 3, 2, 1, and... 0!" they shouted in unison.

"So let the fifth story begin..."

The golden puppy

Timothy could have been an excellent chef. He memorised all of the recipes and enjoyed cooking, but he was a big dreamer. He frequently forgot what he was making and ended up doing something entirely different. He was known to add apple and blueberries to shepherd's pie and cheese and pepper to his scones. He used potatoes instead of pasta, and vice versa. He cooked instead of leavening, and froze the ingredients rather than frying them. He did everything the other way whenever possible.

"Well, my son," the chef said. "This cannot go on any longer. All of my guests will leave. We have to make each dish twice, and not even the pigs will eat your food. You better leave now, because you will never be a chef!"

Timothy's eyes widened, his lips formed an O shape, then he closed and reopened them but ended up saying anything. So he left the restaurant and walked away, looking down. He had no idea where he was going; he just kept walking. He cried at first because he was devastated when the chef told him he would never be a chef. Then he began to fantasise about becoming a hero so famous that the entire world would know his name. He kept thinking about useless things until he arrived at a forest, specifically the deepest part of it. He had no idea how he got there, and to his great dismay, he had no idea where to go from there. So he followed his nose for a while until he saw smoke in the distance. As he got closer, he noticed that it came from a rickety hut with a hole-filled roof. He knocked, and because no one told him to leave, he opened it.

"I got you, hah!" someone shouted.

In the next moment, an ugly, crooked-nosed hag jumped on him. She crossed her legs around his hips, and soon his arms and legs were bound.

"You wandered into the wrong part of the forest," laughed the hag.

She was even uglier when she laughed, which was difficult to accomplish. She bent over a cauldron and threw a variety of herbs into it. Timothy knew what good food smelled like, well, when he wasn't dreaming. He could not help but point out that there was something wrong with the food.

"What on earth are you doing? What is this horrible smell?" he asked.

"Marinade, my dear. I will make it now and rub it on you so you taste better when I eat you."

"No way!" the chef in Timothy was fuming. "That is no marinade. This is horrendous! Even I did nothing like that, not even at my worst."

"What is wrong with my marinade?" asked the hag. "Why? Can you do it better? I heard they kicked you out because you were the worst chef."

Timothy needed no more.

"Listen to me, you ugly hag!" shouted the chef. "I will tell you what good marinade is like. You will not rub me with that stinky whatever."

The hag was surprised because no one had ever talked to her like that before. She started studying Timothy.

"Fine, what do you think I should do?"

"First you throw this slop down the drain, then you take four cloves of garlic, mustard, pepper, carrots," and he went on and on about the recipe.

He was all hyped up. He checked every detail, yelling at the witch if she did something wrong. Meanwhile, she sniffed the marinade. And when it was ready, he grinned in satisfaction.

"You see, this is good stuff. You can marinate me in this."

The hag also smelled and tasted it. She stirred it around as if she were inspecting a delicacy. She didn't want to pour it on Timothy.

"Tell me, what were you using this type of marinade for?"

"This one works best with beef. It enhances the flavour and softens the fibres. "When you cook the meat, it smells like heaven."

Then the witch limped out of the kitchen. There was packing, falling, cursing, and then she appeared, holding a large chunk of beef.

"Here's the beef. Prepare it for me!" She said, removing the rope from Timothy's limbs. "But don't you dare running away, because I will charm you!"

Timothy looked at her, and she did not seem charming at all, so he just shrugged his shoulders. He marinated the beef, and while it was in the liquid, he took out some cards and showed the hag how to play poker. He won a significant amount of money from her because they were playing double. Then he roasted the beef, but as the hag sniffed the food, her nose appeared to shrink. They ate dinner, and the hag promised to eat Timothy the following day because she had already eaten so much today.

They fell asleep and awoke early the next day. The hag announced that she would go shopping and instructed Timothy to get himself cleaned up because she wanted to cook him for lunch. As she wanted to leave the house the chef told her to bring five sprigs of thyme, peppercorns, sage, rosemary, parsley, garlic, Dijon mustard, and lamb's ribs. Everyone deserved a last supper or lunch, and he wanted to eat well-seasoned lamb ribs. The hag opened

her mouth, then closed it, opened it again, and finally left without saying anything.

Timothy was bored, so he went outside and noticed how bad the roof was. He decided to bake sugar-coated gingerbread tiles. He worked fast, the oven was glowing. He began to place them on the roof where the original tiles were missing, and he even installed some on the walls. Finally, he transformed the rickety hut into a stunning gingerbread house. He was putting on the last tiles when the hag arrived. She opened her mouth, surprised, but did not say anything. She handed him the ingredients, and he started working right away. Soon, the delicious-smelling lamb ribs were on the table.

"Don't you want some, old hag?" he asked sweetly.

She devoured the food, having never eaten such a delicacy before. She licked all of her fingers in the end.

"I can't eat you today either, but it is probably for the best. "This was delicious," she said, wiping her mouth.

Timothy looked at her puzzled, because her nose was even smaller and she appeared younger. He just shook his head.

"The house is also beautiful, Timothy. At first, I didn't even recognise it."

As the evening came, they were playing cards once again. Just as Timothy said royal flush, they heard footsteps. The hag went outside and dragged two kids inside by their ears.

"I got you! You could have eaten all the tiles."

"Let us go, you ugly hag!"

"What are your names, little troublemakers?"

"My name is Hansel, and she is my girl Gretel."

"Wait a minute! Isn't Gretel your sister? Whatever! Now I will eat all of you, like I should!"

"Don't be stupid," said Timothy. "You just ate the lamb ribs. I will make you a chocolate soufflé instead."

The soufflé was so delicious that everyone ate multiple bowls of it. They played two rounds of poker after that, but Hansel kept winning, so they didn't want to play any longer. Suddenly, they heard knocking. The hag went to open the door and looked at the visitor with surprise.

"I cannot believe my eyes! What on earth are you doing here?"

She returned with a girl dressed in red.

"She is Little Red Riding Hood," she introduced her. "She was on her way to her grandmother, but the smell was so good that she decided to come here instead."

So it happened that Little Red Riding Hood also ate handsomely from the dinner. Then she got tipsy from the wine they drank afterwards. She told them that she did not like going to her grandmother because her cooking was terrible, but she would like to stay a few more days here if possible. The witch shook her head, because something was not quite right. The world was spinning out of control. Little Red Riding Hood should not be here, and the two naughty children should be in the cauldron. And what was the chef doing here? Meanwhile, Little Red Riding Hood and Timothy went outside for a while and returned holding hands. They clearly liked each other. The hag needed no more. She cried out:

"Everything is different here! Why is everything different?"

Timothy cleared his throat and announced that he wanted to leave with Little Red Riding Hood because they were planning a life together. When they saw the hag's surprised expression, they were on their way. Hansel grabbed Gretel's hand, slapped the hag on the back, and walked to the door.

"Hey, hag!" said Hansel before leaving. "You don't look that bad, by the way."

By the time the hag got over her surprise, she was all alone. She grabbed her mirror, ran her hands through her hair, and smiled at herself.

"I look pretty good. I might call the Wolf for dinner; Little Red Riding Hood left with the chef anyway."

Timothy later opened a restaurant nearby, on the edge of the forest. He created such incredible dishes that people travelled there even from abroad to try them. He became famous. They had seven children, seven little dwarves, but that is another story.

And what about the golden puppy? Where is he? Did we forget about him? Of course not! He was in my lap the entire time. But he fell asleep, and I didn't want to wake him. He is stretching his legs right now.

"But Pop, you mixed up everything in this story," laughed Pete.

"You even added the seven dwarves. Don't you know the tales?" said Judy.

"Okay, fine. I did mix them. But this is the story of a chef who creates new recipes."

"And what about the puppy? You said there would be a puppy."

"I didn't say that. I only said we'd see. But the puppy was in my lap, wasn't he? I said it."

"I liked it better this way," said Mum. "It was different from the classic stories."

They spent a lot of time talking about the puppy and what happened that day. But night proved stronger than them, and they all fell asleep, including Pop.

Day Six

Pete and Judy raced down the stairs. There was no more guessing what the breakfast would be; they knew it would be delicious either way. That morning, they had cinnamon rolls, and they drank milk. However, there were bacon, fried eggs, and grilled tomatoes on the dining table too. Mum was, once again, taken aback by the children's appetites.

Pop announced that they will go to the arboretum. Pete and Judy had no idea what it was, but they were still excited. Mum drove because the arboretum was a little farther away and they needed to take the car. They sang, joked, and laughed all the way there.

When they entered the arboretum, Pop told them that there are many fascinating plants and animals to see. They saw a variety of evergreens, including Leyland cypress, northern white cedar, and several emerald green pine trees. There were huge, old English oaks and plants from all over the world with names they could not pronounce no matter how hard they tried. Then they gathered around a centuries-old tree with a trunk so thick that when they formed a chain, their hands barely touched.

They fed the deer and European roe, then observed the hedgehogs and birds. Papa wanted to stop by every tree, but the kids were more interested in the animals. They were exhausted by the time they arrived at the arboretum trail's end. They headed home because Papa wanted to have a barbecue in the garden. The kids' stomachs were already growling, and it was not even noon. They made sausages and chicken breasts, and it smelled incredible.

They ate everything and licked their fingers at the end. Mum complained that her mouth had cramped up since they had been at Papa's because she had been smiling so much.

The afternoon playtime dragged on, and it was getting dark by the time they were ordered into the house. They ate quickly and then rushed to the bathroom, afraid they would be late and miss the story. But the story was not missed. They quickly reported:

"Traveller Judy is ready for the tale."

"Traveller Pete is ready for the tale."

"Traveller Mum is ready for the tale."

Then the well-known countdown started.

"10, 9, 8, 7, 6, 5, 4, 3, 2, 1, and... 0!" they shouted in unison.

"And so the sixth story begins..."

The Portrait

In the high mountains of Finland, where the wind blows and everything is covered in snow and ice. Oh, no! Brrr. It's too cold there. It's not good.

Then let it be in France. On Paris's small, narrow streets, where water always runs along the pavement carrying trash, while cars exhaust... No! We don't want to wander around smoky, smelly streets. But then, where?

Leylandia, as the sun rose and warmed the trees' leaves. That is more like it. Leylandia it is.

Leylandia was a small kingdom with large fields, grazing animals, a mill by the stream, and people rushing about. The royal palace stood atop the hill, surrounded by guards. Not because the people in the country wanted to harm the king, but because every kingdom had a large number of guards, and King Gideon II was careful not to be outdone by other kings.

His son, the young prince, spent the entire day studying important subjects such as state formation, kingdom administration, constitutional studies, wine science, and ballroom dancing. He learned a variety of skills that he would never use in real life. And, while he could not hammer a nail into a wall, he knew which year of champagne was the most delicious, and he could dance most of the dances fairly well. It is understandable that, with all of his knowledge, he would make little progress if stranded on a desert island. However, he had no intention of moving to such a location, preferring to follow in his father's footsteps as King Jeremiah III.

Because his studies did not bind him down too much, he had plenty of free time to learn to imitate birds, then various domestic animals, and even a few wild ones. Finally, he observed the people around him and imitated the commander of the guard and even the king with great accuracy, much to the delight of the court servants. But after a while, he became bored, and one day, while walking around the palace grounds, he discovered the forge. He hid, and from his hiding place, he watched the sweating blacksmith who used his muscular arms to make weapons, knives, axes, and other iron objects. He was fascinated by the sight, and knew at once that he would have to learn to do it himself.

"In the name of the King," he said, using the guard commander's voice.

The blacksmith jumped to his feet, but he was so tall that he hit his head on the ceiling beam. He wailed while holding his head in both hands.

Prince Jeremiah began laughing and slapping his knees. Until the blacksmith slapped him hard enough to make his ears ring. He fell silent, then got very angry.

"What are you doing, servant? Can't you see you're standing before your prince?" he asked.

The blacksmith covered his mouth, unable to believe his ears, and knelt on the ground, stammering:

"Forgive me, my prince. Your father could have taught you manners, or something useful," he added quietly.

The prince overheard him and was about to say something nasty to the arrogant subject when he noticed a dagger. He liked it so much that he forgot all about the prank.

"Get up, good man," he said earnestly to the blacksmith, "I want you to teach me how to make weapons."

"My prince, this is not a job for you. Just go hunt and have fun. This is hard work."

"I would like to learn it," Jeremiah said again, and the fire in his eyes made Claus, the blacksmith, smile.

"Very well," he agreed. "But then you are no longer a prince here, and I am no longer a subject. You will be a servant, and I will be your master."

The prince agreed immediately, and they began training that same day. Claus explained how to light a fire, how to feed it with the bellows, how to turn iron ore into glowing metal, and the steps to shaping it into a horseshoe, knife, sword, or nail. As they progressed, he taught the prince mathematics and geometry, how to make armour, the mysteries of keys and locks, and how to open any door. In addition to winemaking, he was starting to learn some practical skills that would keep him from starving to death on that desert island. All of this physical work strengthened his arms, firmed his pecs, and broadened his shoulders. We have to say, he grew into quite a sturdy lad. Claus looked at him, patted him on the shoulder, and then, with a sudden movement, hugged him tightly and whispered in his ear:

"You are ready, my son. Nobody can defeat you now," he said, not realising how much his words made Jeremiah blush.

The king was not pleased to learn that his son was going to the blacksmith in addition to his court lessons, but he was preoccupied with the kingdom's problems. They were almost entirely in debt. They had hardly any money left. In order to strengthen his financial position, he negotiated with other kingdoms to marry off his son, the heir to his throne. So they could get out of this trouble with a rich princess and her dowry. He found his future daughter-in-law and her prosperous kingdom, Emeraldia. He requested a picture of the Princess of Emeraldia. When the portrait arrived, he summoned his son, had a photograph taken of him, and sent it to Emerald.

When the prince arrived, his father informed him that he had found the perfect wife for him. He showed the portrait to Jeremiah.

"Oh, my dear!" the prince exclaimed. "Who is this hag? Well, I'm not going to marry her, that's for sure!" said the prince. He threw the picture to the ground and stomped on it.

"This is not a request programme," the king stated. "What is wrong with this girl?" he asked, picking up the slightly battered picture. "Oh, gross!" he blurted out.

He shut his eyes, then opened them again.

"This is truly awful," he said. "But she has a lot of money!"

"My dear father," said Jeremiah. "Please do not make me marry this witch. This picture is so ugly that if I showed it to the kids in the kingdom, they would be weeping for weeks."

But the king was adamant. When he saw the picture, his stomach turned, but he ordered his son to marry her for the sake of the country. He dashed out of the room and slammed the door, locking it from the outside to keep the prince from fleeing. Jeremiah sat for a while, cursing fate for making him a prince, before realising he had learned the magic of locks. He pulled out the skeleton key and was free in no time. He ran to the blacksmith, asked him for bad clothes, and ran to the town gate.

However, it was guarded by many men that day. So Jeremiah hid, and imitating the voice of the guard commander, directed the soldiers to the other gate. Thanks to the chaos, he was soon on the other side of the gate.

He was running, with no idea where he was going, when he heard that he was being chased by dogs. His lungs were burning, and no matter how fit he was, he felt he could not run much longer. That's when he spotted the dock, where a ship was being loaded. They were just finishing up work, and the captain was directing the men when the prince jumped on board behind him. However, the guards noticed him and were getting closer and closer. Jeremiah panicked and cried out, imitating the captain's voice.

"Anchor up! Unfurl the sails! Full speed ahead!"

The crew acted quickly, and by the time the guards arrived to the shore, the ship was already a hundred yards away. Despite the chaos on board, the captain had a valid reason not to turn back: they were pirates. Although he was relieved they were off, he could not figure out why they had left port.

"You were the one who said: 'Anchor up!', my captain," said one of the sailors, then hurried off to do his job.

The captain was thinking for days but only realised what had happened later.

Jeremiah hid in the hold, where he had everything he needed to survive the journey. There was water, food, and even a mattress. He also discovered an armour. Which started talking out of nowhere just as he was about to throw it away. Then he found out that armour was, in fact, inhabited. When Jeremiah asked what he was doing there, the armour told him the whole story.

"So, when I was a little kid," began the owner of the armour, Wolfgang.

Then he had to skip a longer section because Jeremiah threatened to slap him if he did not get to the point.

"So, my grandfather Wolfgang painted portraits. Like the rest of the family, he went by Wolfgang. So I became a portrait painter as well, but one of my last pieces turned out to be quite bad. So I decided it was best to disappear. I went to the museum to hide, but then I heard they were looking for me and saw the armour."

"And? Could you please speed things up?" Jeremiah stood up, ready to slap the armoured man.

"So, I tried on the armour in the museum," said Wolfgang. "But it was too small, and I couldn't take it off ever since."

After he learned almost the whole story, they had lunch. They got along well, eating and drinking a lot, and having conversations, but after a while, the journey became boring.

The captain was nervously pacing the deck, because there had been no wind for days and they had made very little progress. The sailors also reported that they were running low on food and water, as if they had not packed enough. People were getting angry because the portions needed to be cut. The captain refused to believe it because he had calculated the amount they needed for the trip himself and had never been incorrect. As he became more and more nervous, he heard loud shouting. Two sailors appeared with a strange duo. By the way he was dressed, one had to be a blacksmith, a strong, muscular lad, while the other fellow was wearing armour.

"Captain, we have the two culprits who are scavenging our food. That's why we are running out. What shall we do with them? Hang them, or shoot them in the head?"

The captain considered the two options because he liked both. But in the end, he ordered that they be tied together and thrown into the sea.

"Can't you do something? They look like they are about to throw us into the sea. I'm too young for that. Look at me! Wouldn't it be a pity?"

The prince looked at him.

"Not really," he said, and as the other kept crying, he shouted at him: "Shut your mouth. Can't you be quiet for a moment?"

Taking advantage of the brief silence, he turned his head and shouted loudly in the voice of one of the sailors: "Land to the North-East!"

Despite their hunger and thirst, the sailors gathered on the opposite side of the ship, looking for land, but finding none. However, the captain's face lit up.

"So you were the one giving the orders when we set off. I must admit it was clever. Now you will have plenty of time to imitate the fish!"

And once again, he gave the order to throw them into the sea. However, just as they were trying to lift their tied-up bodies over the rail, the sailor in the crow's nest shouted:

"Land on the horizon!"

They were turning their heads left and right until they noticed the thin line on the horizon. Everyone cheered. The hitchhikers were not thrown into the sea at the end, but when they moored, they were chased to the shore with loud laughter.

The strange duo set out for the town, talking along the way. The sun was blazing hard, and the armour was becoming hotter. Wolfgang eyed Jeremiah, then began to beg him:

"Listen, I can't keep this costume on me anymore. I'm sweating like a pig. Can't you take it off?"

The prince looked at the armour and, having learned all the tricks of the trade, quickly took out a hammer, chisel, and various tools to free Wolfgang from the hot and tight cage. But he regretted it right away because the heat and lack of proper washing made him smell rather unpleasant.

"I don't want to compliment you," he said. "But you smell pretty bad. I will either put you back into the armour or you will wash yourself at this well in an instant."

When the now-armourless portrait painter saw his serious expression, he chose an ice-cold bath instead.

"Now you can come with me."

When they arrived in town, chaos greeted them. Everyone was looking for a blacksmith to help free the king's daughter, who got stuck in her closet and no one could open the lock. The barker even offered a reward of a hundred gold coins in the name of the King of Emeraldia. When Jeremiah heard this, he wanted to run away because he remembered how ugly the girl looked in the picture.

"Don't you want to help?" asked Wolfgang

"Let the executioner help her! If you saw her in the painting, you would not rush to her either."

"I think you should give it a try," said Wolfgang, who immediately put it all together in his head.

Then, as the prince headed for the palace, he ran back to the harbour, eager to leave the country as soon as possible. The prince pushed aside the various helpers, who had all failed. He put an end to catastrophe tourism, as many people enjoyed listening to the princess' weeping. He went to the closet and shouted:

"Be quiet, you hag! Damn those tramps! They get stuck everywhere! You'd rather stay inside!"

He fiddled with the lock for a while, then it let go, and Jeremiah held his breath, waiting for the ugly girl to come out. However, the hideously ugly girl didn't come out, as she was never inside. The princess shook her head, her red hair swaying back and forth. She fixed her blue eyes on Jeremiah, her face freckled and her lips a stunning red.

"Who is the hag?" she asked, putting her hands on her hips.

Jeremiah was about to suffocate, partly because he had stopped breathing, but mostly because of the princess' breath-taking beauty. Then he remembered that maybe he shouldn't suffocate and began breathing rapidly. He would have panted anyway because his heart was pounding so loud with love that they could hear it from the street.

"Who is the hag?" asked the princess again.

However, she did not continue because she also liked the guy a lot. He was toned, with sun-kissed abs and curly hair. He was a charming lad, for sure.

"Who are you?" she asked in a hushed voice.

So Jeremiah told the whole adventure. Then he asked who the hag in the picture was, and the princess assured him that she was her father's only daughter. And as Jeremiah listened to her, the entire situation became increasingly suspicious. He apologised and promised to return soon, then ran back to Wolfgang, but he was nowhere to be found. After searching everywhere, he found him in the harbour. He squeezed him tightly and promised to keep doing so until he was out of breath if the painter did not tell him everything.

Wolfgang admitted that every picture he sold was painted by his grandfather. However, he fell ill just as the king ordered the portrait, so he had to paint the princess himself.

"I'm not to blame for how it turned out," he cried.

The prince went back to his country and told his father that he had thought it over and was going to go ahead with the marriage. His father was so relieved, he didn't even ask where he had been. However, when the veil was removed from the princess's head at the wedding, the king laughed and looked at his son. Jeremiah winked, walked up to the princess, and kissed her. But no one could see it because the veil was covering them.

And what happened to the armoured man? Wolfgang was appointed curator of the Royal Picture Gallery. It was made a law that no one could ever put paint or brushes in his hands, and anyone who broke it would face life in prison. Let's admit, it was a wise decision.

"Pop, didn't that type of cypress we saw in the arboretum today have the same name as the kingdom in the story?" asked Mum.

"Well, maybe," laughed Pop. "The story could have happened anywhere. But yes, the idea came from the cypress."

"I saw the whole thing in front of me as you were telling it. It was like watching a movie," said Judy.

"Maybe they should make a movie out of it," said Mum.

They spent so much time talking about Leylandia and Emeraldia that they forgot to ask Pop to repeat the story. By the time they realised they were already half asleep, they soon slipped into slumberland.

Mom kept asking Papa where he got these stories, but Papa couldn't tell her. He said they just came to him. Then Mum fell asleep as well.

Day Seven

The numerous things they did the day before paid off, as the kids awoke later today. When they came down from upstairs, the dining table was filled with sausages, baked beans, harsh brown, boiled eggs, mushrooms and grilled tomatoes. There was orange juice and milk in pitchers. Mum was looking at it in awe.

"Dad, this would be enough for a whole army."

"But here are the little soldiers," laughed Pop, lifting the kids in the air one by one, turning them around, then putting them in the chairs. "Eat up, drink up! You'll need the energy."

They went to see the nearby castle, which was recently renovated. Pete and Judy loved the fully furnished rooms, the old furniture and clothes. They imagined themselves as princes and princesses, dancing in the ballroom. At the end of the exhibition, they dressed up in costumes, and Mum and Pop took pictures of them. They were like children of the aristocracy from the past.

Then they went outside to the gardens and ran around in the grass. They went to the pond and crossed the small bridge to the island in the centre. They even got two scoops of ice cream each, which they ate while walking back to the car. On the way home, they could not stop talking. They asked about what it was like back in the day when there were kings and queens and what the kids did, and Pop answered every question.

They had shepherd's pie for lunch and French onion soup beforehand. Pete and Judy dug in eagerly. Mum was as amazed as she had been every day.

"You don't even like French onion soup."

"Oh, that's right," laughed Judy. "But we like it here."

Pete ate the soup without saying anything; his thoughts were elsewhere. Then Pop and Mum cut the pie and the kids both ate two slices. They talked a little more while sitting at the table, but then the kids noticed something interesting in the garden and ran outside to play. Mum helped Pop wash the dishes and clean the kitchen.

It was a long summer day, and the sun never seemed to set, but the kids were exhausted after running all day. Mum had a hard time getting them in the bathtub.

"Can't we just skip the bath today?" asked Pete. "We'll do it in the morning."

But Mum was adamant. They went into the bath pouting a little, but then quickly forgot they were grumpy. They pulled the blanket over themselves, finally clean, their hair still a bit damp.

"Now, let me see my travellers!" said Pop. "Let's check the attendance!"

"To Captain Pop, I report that Traveller Pete is ready for the tale!"

"To Captain Pop, I report that Traveller Judy is ready for the tale!"

"Good," smiled Pop, then he turned to Mum. "Now you."

"Fine, then I'll report too. To Captain Pop, I report that Traveller Mum is ready for the tale"

Then they did the countdown together.

"10, 9, 8, 7, 6, 5, 4, 3, 2, 1, and... 0!"

"And so the seventh story begins..."

The Village Idiot

Tobias and Timothy were brothers. However, no one has ever seen a more distinct pair of brothers. Timothy was always a rowdy, loud-mouthed, boisterous lad, whereas Tobias was a soft-spoken boy who always smiled goofily. They kept nudging Tobias to speak, but he just smiled and said, "I will speak when I have something important to say." Timothy, on the other hand, was chatting away and making everyone laugh; people adored him. No wonder Tobias was referred to as the village idiot behind his back. He was a bright kid, but he rarely spoke and always had a big grin on his face. He really did look like an idiot. Not even a little. The boys and girls laughed at him, and perhaps even the dogs. Okay, the dogs didn't. Moreover! Every animal was quite fond of him. When he walked down the street, they all followed him one by one. The dogs were barking happily, the geese honked, and the bees buzzed, but they also stung him afterwards to keep him from getting ahead of himself. Even Timothy laughed at him, but Tobias was a good brother and never got mad at him. He loved everybody, but nobody loved him.

One day, the two brothers went fishing. They cast their lines and waited. Timothy was whistling, while Tobias smiled at the fish, water, wind, trees, and frogs. It is easier to say that he always smiled at everyone because it was a part of his personality. When he caught a fish, he would remove the hook from its mouth, kiss it on the head, and throw it back into the water. Then came the next one, followed by another fish, and so on. Catch, kiss, and throw back.

"What on earth are you doing?" asked Timothy, who couldn't even catch a tadpole. "Why are you throwing back every fish? In the end, we'll starve to death."

But Tobias just smiled and continued fishing. As his brother lay back in the grass, his bobber suddenly sank, indicating that there was something big on the hook. He pulled it from the water, but it was a turtle, not a fish. As he pressed a kiss on his head, the shell began speaking. Timothy only noticed that Tobias was speaking. So he turned to him because it was a rare occasion, and then he realised he was talking with a turtle.

"Okay, but what should I wish for?" asked Tobias.

It was an unusual scene as he spoke to the wrinkled turtle. But the turtle responding was even more peculiar. Timothy shook his head; he couldn't believe what he was seeing.

"Whatever you want," the turtle told Tobias, who, for the first time in his life, had a cloudy expression.

"I wish for a ladder, as long as I want it to be."

"As you wish," said the turtle.

Now, Timothy was truly astonished.

"Now, wait a minute. My dear brother, my flesh and blood, my only true kinsman, I hear you're about to make a wish. I don't understand why it's not a goldfish, but a turtle who's talking, but whatever. I can't believe it! But what's my precious brother's wish? Huh? A ladder! Well, I'll just override that like the senior wisher. So we need a lot of money, so much that even my grandchildren can't spend it."

At this, the turtle looked at Timothy. His eyes unblinking, his gaze penetrating, then averted his eyes.

"Come on, Tobias, what are your other two wishes? But only you can wish your brother can fish himself another turtle."

"Okay, then I want wings I can fly with," he said with a dreamy look.

"What the... Are you crazy or something? Money, money! Wish for money, for heaven's sake!" shouted his brother.

"And then my third wish will be..."

"Money, money, moneeeeey!" screamed Timothy.

"So, I will wish for a fig tree that has fruit on it the whole year."

Timothy fell to the ground and began beating it with both hands, berating Tobias in the process. He wept and moaned, but nothing could be done. Three wishes are three wishes, not four or five. The turtle made his way to the water with slow steps. Tobias held a small ladder, tiny wings, and one fig in his hands.

"What have you done? You village idiot!" Timothy scolded his brother. "We could have been rich!"

"Listen, bro. You didn't hear the beginning, right? The turtle said I can't ask for money or a long life."

Timothy stiffened briefly before regaining his composure and explaining that he still wished for stupid things. He could have asked for lottery winnings, stock market advice, or simply a trip to the future, but Tobias' smile returned and he could not be talked about it any longer. He caught twenty-three more fish, you know, the animals loved him, but then Timothy got fed up as he caught nothing and suggested going home instead.

As the days passed, word spread that the King's daughter had reached the marriageable age, and suitors came from all over the world. The Main Street was packed with princes, earls, and barons vying for the princess' hand, but the clever princess assigned tasks and puzzles that none of the suitors could solve. The king became more and more angry and summoned his daughter.

"Now, listen to me, my daughter. You are no longer a young fräulein; you are about to turn thirty-two, and you have yet to find a husband. I am dying to be a grandfather, so why are you assigning them tasks that no one can complete?"

"But Daddy, I want the person who wins my hand to be worthy of it."

"All right, but you will need to order some anti-wrinkle lotion soon because those hands are getting old," the king fumed.

Then he had a thought and announced to the country that, instead of royal suitors, whoever solved her daughter's puzzles could marry her. They might even get some money.

Timothy heard this and rushed to Tobias, telling him that they finally had a chance to go from rags to riches. He persuaded his brother to apply for the royal son-in-law's position. They were waiting for the first task. The next day, the princess stepped out onto the balcony and announced the day's task. Timothy's smile faded because the princess was so stunning that the birds stopped singing in envy. They didn't actually shut up, but the princess still looked quite stunning, just enough to make Jiminy go completely white, panting and stuttering. People began laughing when they saw Tobias, the village idiot. Tobias simply smiled, but Timothy became even paler as the princess requested a golden rod. It would not have been a big deal, but this damn golden rod was growing on top of a sky-high tree guarded by a giant bird. The suitors, both rich and poor, were unable to climb more than the first ten feet of the tree trunk.

Timothy just scratched his head, but Tobias pulled out the ladder the turtle had given him. The ladder continued to grow until it was so long that they could not see the end of it. Tobias climbed up it, but he also started a lift that was somehow on the side of the ladder, and soon he was at the top of the tree that reached the sky. It was so cold at the top that he almost froze. He wanted to break the golden rod, but the giant bird appeared and flapped its wings so hard that Tobias almost fell to the ground. He then remembered his second wish and took out the wings, attaching them to himself. He broke off the golden rod and leapt into the air. The giant bird attempted to fly after him, but Tobias was faster. He soon landed and gave Timothy the rod, which he proudly presented to the princess.

The princess accepted it, but she was furious. On the one hand, she didn't think anyone would succeed, and on the other, she didn't think it would be such a handsome lad.

She pondered for a long time before deciding to ask for a silver fig, which no one could possibly bring her because they only grow in the land of giants. Even Tobias was upset by this news, as he had run out of ideas. He and Timothy set off in search of the figs with their heads down, so much so that they did not notice it until they arrived in the land of the giants. The giants caught them and took them to the Giant King, and told him that these two little intruders had crossed the border of their land. The king of the giants immediately threw them into a dungeon to be cooked into soup the next day. As they sat on death row, they heard weeping outside. They climbed to the window and saw a giant girl outside, the daughter of the king of giants.

"Why are you crying, little girl?" asked Tobias.

A strange thing to ask from a giant.

"Because I love figs so much, but they do not grow here."

"Now, wait a moment," said Timothy. "They told us silver figs grow here."

"Well, maybe they used to, a long time ago. But now we have no figs," and she started crying again.

"Oh, don't cry, little girl," said Tobias kindly.

Then he gave her the fig he got from the turtle. The giant girl's face lit up and she took the fruit. As she was munching on it, the seeds fell to the ground. And behold, a miracle! They started growing in an instant and became silver fig trees. Timothy's eyes grew wide, and he realised they only had to get out of there and the princess would be his. So he asked the giant girl to be so kind, and let them out. Then he took one of the figs and was already on his way. But Tobias didn't follow him.

"Come on, you idiot," said Timothy.

But Tobias was sitting in the giant princess' palm, staring at her with love, just as she did at him. It was a strange sight to see a giant girl and a happy little dwarf lost in each other's eyes. Timothy let out a sigh and took the silver fig to the royal court. The princess gaped and gazed, mainly at the handsome lad, and did not want to give him any more tasks; all she wanted was to marry him. Timothy was happy, firstly because he finally became rich and secondly because he also liked the princess very much. And as he proposed to her, Tobias also popped the question to the giant princess. He became the king of gi-ants, and every giant respected him as he was a wise king.

Nobody called him the village idiot anymore, and he was also very close to the giant girl's heart, in her pocket!

"I thought Tobias will marry the princess," said Pete.

"Well, he did. He married the giant princess."

"Pop, everything is different in your stories," laughed Judy.

"My stories are like that."

"You will tell it again, right?" asked Pete.

After Pop told them again they talked a bit about the turtle who was like a goldfish and they imagined as the giant princess was keeping her husband in her pocket. They had a good laugh about that. Pop couldn't be persuaded to tell the story a third time. So they tucked themselves in, got a good-night kiss and soon fell asleep.

Mum chatted to Pop for a while on the veranda, with a blanket draped over her back. Then she got sleepy too, and the house went quiet, each tale traveller dreaming their own story.

Day Eight

In the morning, when the kids woke up to the delicious smell coming from the kitchen, there was a steaming cup of hot tea in front of Mum. It had a delicate vanilla scent.

"Can we have some, Mum?"

"Sure, this is rooibos tea, you can drink some."

Pop continued the baking fresh scones that he and Mum put together early in the morning. The clotted cream, all types of jams and powdered sugar were already on the table.

They put them on the warm scones, and both kids had a few of them.

"Oh, my tummy is going to explode," said Pete, laughing.

"Mine has already exploded," joked Judy.

After breakfast, Pop announced that they were going to the beach again today. Of course, they will find a place with some shade. It would be unfair to go home without swimming in the lake. Mum put sunscreen on them and a hat on their heads. She laid on the towel to get some sun while Pop was reading a book. But the peace was short-lived, as the kids discovered a little water snake and started shouting for everyone to come and see what they had found. Not far from them, a few tadpoles swam in the lake, a lazy frog jumped into the water. The beach was full of things to explore. The warm water tickled their ankles.

Pop found a few good pebbles and taught them stone skipping. Pete's bounced three times on the water, while Judy's only bounced twice. She instantly started pouting, but Pop assured her that she would be as good as his brother next year. Later, they went back to the house, and Pop and Mum made lunch. They all had plenty to eat, then spent the afternoon in the garden.

"Dad, will you tell a new story today?"

"Well, of course. I already have one in mind," said Pop.

"But where do you get them from?"

"From everywhere. The things I see, the things I hear, from old stories that come to mind, sometimes I just make them up on the spot."

As the evening drew on, this time Mum was the most excited about this night's tale-travel. The kids were happily splashing in the bathtub, then they came in their pyjamas and started chanting:

"We want a story, we want a story, we want a story!"

"Good, good, but you know this isn't how it works. Where is the report?"

So all the travellers reported to Captain Pop.

"Traveller Judy is ready for the tale!"

"Traveller Pete is ready for the tale!"

"Traveller Mum, I'm ready for the tale as well!"

Of course, they couldn't skip the joint countdown either.

"10, 9, 8, 7, 6, 5, 4, 3, 2, 1 and... 0!" they shouted in unison.

"Then the eighth story begins..."

Tea O'Clock

ord Rooibos was crying as he sipped on his afternoon tea. Oh, wait... Just a minute. Lord Pullington was sipping on his rooibos tea as he cried. No, stop. Something is wrong. Once again. Lord Pullington was writing his rooibos tea while he was crying. No, it's still not quite right. So, once again, on Rooibos Street, Lord Pullington was drinking his Earl Grey while... while he was writing. Yes, this is it! So let's start the story.

"Come in!" said the Lord when someone knocked on the door. He looked up as a man walked into the room and, after a brief pause, set down the letter he had just begun writing.

"Please, sit down, Mr..."

"Eddington, at your service, Private Detective Eddington."

"Ah, of course. Mr. Eddington. Well, I asked you to come here because of certain unfortunate—"

"Oh, yes. I've heard Lord Pullington. Your daughter has gone missing. Please, tell me what happened."

"Well, Mr. Eddington, I would appreciate it if you did not cut me off. My daughter went to university, but she has not responded to my letters in three months, nor has she visited the university."

"Do you have a picture of her?"

Lord Pullington began rummaging through his wallet, eventually pulling out a slightly yellow photograph and handing it to the detective.

"How old is your daughter?"

"She is just over twenty-four."

"Well, only because there is a three-month-old baby in this picture. Do you happen to have a more recent photo?"

"No, but trust me, she hasn't changed much."

With that, the Lord sent him on his way. As the detective stepped outside, he looked at the little white clouds and furrowed his brows. Never before had he begun a case with such a small lead. Then he shrugged his shoulders and began searching for Livia Pullington, who appeared to be a three-month-old baby, which was rather unusual for a university student.

His first trip was to the university because he considered himself a good detective and thought it was a logical place to start. Nobody knew where she went. He questioned her classmates, professors, and even the receptionist, but to no avail. As she really could be anywhere, he decided to go to the railway station and get on the first train. There was still time before departure, so he went to a nearby café and ordered a cup of tea with a splash of milk. He drank it standing next to the counter, as detectives do, and then took out the photograph to show the waiter.

"Do you recognise this woman?"

"Well, I don't know if it really is a woman because of the diaper, but now I cannot say I do."

"She is twenty-four and her name is Livia Pullington."

"Oh, now I can see it," said the waiter, seemingly relieved. "You should ask the hag."

"What hag?"

"Well, the crooked-handed, long-nosed old hag who lives in the Lenderville Woods.

"Thank you. You helped a lot."

Detective Gustav Eddington shook the held-out hand of the waiter.

"Actually, I was asking for the money for the coffee," croaked the boy.

"Oh, of course, here you go, son," said the detective, handing him a pound, then, seeing his scowl another one. "The rest is yours."

Then he gracefully crumpled the bill with two pounds and twenty pence written on it, tossed it on the table, and exited the café.

Lenderville was in the mountains, surrounded by such dense forest that he was entangled in branches and thorns with each step. By the time the path became clearer, he had to hold his trousers up to keep them from falling. When he arrived at the neat little hut with a smoking chimney and inviting lights in its windows, his clothes were a little battered and his skin was covered in scratches. He knocked on the door, and as soon as he was let in, he realised that what they had said in the café was not entirely accurate. The hag wasn't nearly as ugly as they had described her. No. She was much uglier. Her fingers ended in sharp, pointy nails that resembled a hawk's claws. But her nose! Well, it was pretty big. Or rather, bigger than pretty. She smiled to appear more charming, but whoever gave her this advice did not mean well.

"Come in, son! Sit down, warm up a little," she said, and her voice wasn't any better than her smile. "The soup is almost ready."

As soon as Gustav smelled the soup, he forgot everything else. He did not care who cooked it or where he was; he began gobbling it up eagerly. He had to admit that he had never tasted such a delicious soup before. He asked for a refill twice before wiping his mouth and looking at the hag. However, it was not the best thing to do after eating.

"Ma'am," he began politely, as he was always a gentleman. "I'm looking for Livia Pullington, who disappeared from her university. They said you're the only one who could help me."

"Yes, oh yes," nodded the long-nosed hag. "But why would I tell you?"

"Well, because if you don't, I will not receive any money from the Lord, which would be a significant financial loss for me."

The hag laughed and adjusted her bonnet after a few strands of hair escaped. She looked in the mirror to see if she was pretty enough. Something was probably wrong with the mirror because she seemed pleased as she sat down in front of the man. She took his hand and abruptly turned it, which caught the detective off guard. She started to examine Gustav's palm, then let go of it.

"Now, my son. I can see in your palm that you are a good man. I will tell you that pirates kidnapped Livia Pullington and are currently holding her hostage in a small hut in the mountains. I'll also tell you how to find it if you promise me something."

"Ask for anything. If I can, I'll make it true."

"You have to because I only need a candelabra. If you do not bring it, you will never return to the Lord. Promise me that you will bring it."

"Yes, I promise, just tell me where the house is."

"There is a path here, behind the hut. You take it, and when it branches, stay to the left because the one on the right leads directly into the ravine. Then, when it branches again, stay on the right because the one on the left leads directly into the ravine. When it splits into three, do not take either of the side paths; instead, stay in the middle.

"Thank you. Then I'll be on my way."

"Don't be in such a hurry. You can leave in the morning."

And so he did, but as the detective was about to leave, the hag handed him three kernels of corn and told him to take care of them.

"But what am I supposed to do with these corn kernels?"

"You'll figure it out in time," she said.

And Gustav set off down the path.

The road was long, but he followed the hag's directions, and as it got dark, he used a flashlight to keep his eyes on the road. He arrived at the second crossroads at dawn, and the third in the early afternoon. From there, the road led straight to the house of the alleged pirates.

"Easy peasy," he thought to himself. "I go in, get the girl, and return her to the Lord, and the case is solved."

As he reached this point in his train of thought, he was interrupted by a startling creature.

Gustav Eddington turned pale, having never seen a three-headed chicken the size of a horse. Furthermore, each of the heads had a beak that was constantly snapping at him, as if attempting to catch a tasty treat. He starched his head because it seemed like he could neither get around the hen – or hens, if you count the number of heads – nor run past it or them. He was furious, wondering how such a creature had gotten here, and as he slapped his leg in anger, he felt the hard seeds in his pocket. He took them out, and the hen saw this and wanted to get them right away.

"Now, wait a minute! I am going to trick you, all of you somehow."

Then he took three kernels of corn and threw them in three different directions.

The hen did not need any more and tried to catch them. Sure enough, but each head chose a different corn. This was beyond her abilities, and the hen collapsed on her belly, banged all her heads, and fainted. Gustav quickly ran past them. The pirates were so confident in the three-headed giant hen's protection that they did not even have a guard. He crept carefully into the house, looking for Livia.

He finally found her upstairs, sitting on the balcony. He dashed up to her, but instead of a three-month-old baby's face, he was greeted by a beautiful lady with a crown of black hair. The face was accompanied by lips that formed a surprising shape of O. She asked what he was doing there.

Master Detective Gustav Eddington told her that her father sent him. Wondering the whole time, how can someone be so gorgeous.

"You are very sweet," she said, and she truly meant it, because Gustav was not an unpleasant man either, but there is no getting away from here. A three-headed hen guards the farm and has a habit of smashing everyone's head who tries to get past her.

Gustav looked out the window and saw that the hen heads were still lying on the ground, unconscious. He motioned for the girl to hurry. But as they were leaving the house, he remembered he needed to take the wretched candelabra with him. He told her to stay where she was and ran back into the house.

Oh yes, but the candelabra was on the table where the pirates were sitting, getting ready for dinner. It seemed hopeless to take it without being noticed. He ran back to Livia and instructed her to make a loud noise in twenty seconds. So she did. The pirates ran out, and Gustav quickly blew out the candle. In the darkness, the pirates bumped into each other. Gustav gripped her hand tightly, and they ran towards the chicken. Meanwhile, the bird-giant awoke, spotted them, and attacked. However, it was still dizzy and could not see well in the dark, so each of its attacks hit the ground next to them, leaving a small crater. They were running fast, and Gustav waited a long time before turning on the flashlight. But just in time, because they were standing right on the edge of the ravine. They were terrified, but Gustav, who had not become a master detective by chance, realised that this was the ravine on the

left. So they changed directions and had to go left because their backs were turned to what was in front of them on the way here. Because he was an extremely clever man. They found the path and arrived at the hag's hut by late afternoon. Just as they walked in, the hag demanded to know where the candelabra was.

"Wait a minute, you old hag," scolded her Gustav. "I have it with me. But why do you need it?"

"Is it any of your business? Just give it to me! That was the deal."

With trembling hands, she greedily grabbed it from his grip.

She placed it on the table, lit it, and stared at the flame for a while before taking out a mirror. The detective and the girl had no idea what was going on. But as time passed, the old hag grew younger, slowly at first, then faster. Her hair blackened, her claws vanished, and her face became more attractive. But the real surprise was when she turned around. She looked eerily like Livia.

"Mother?" She marvelled and sprang to the hag, who wasn't really a hag anymore; she looked more like the wife of a lord. They embraced and cried for a long time.

Then they told how, when Livia was a little child, her mother had disappeared. The pirates' wizard cursed her to live as a hag for eternity unless a young man brought them the pirates' candelabra, in the light of which she could see herself in the mirror again.

They quickly set off and returned to their manor on Rooibos Street. There was a great celebration in the Lord's house because not only his daughter but also his wife had returned. Master Detective Gustav Eddington also received his reward, they paid him handsomely. They even invited him to tea, where he had a long conversation with Livia. According to some unverified sources, the tea was so well received that it ended in a wedding, but this could all have been a fairy tale.

"Dad! Isn't this rooibos the tea we had this morning?" Mum scolded Pop.

"Of course not!!! There is a street like this in Antwerp. I looked it up," whispered Pop to Mum.

"I wouldn't want to meet a hen that big," said Pete. "I'm already scared of the normal-sized ones."

"Pop, tell it again!" asked Judy.

So Pop told the story again, just like he always did. The kids laughed at different things than the previous time. Mum also loved the story and wanted to be the one to ask Pop to tell it again, but she didn't.

"Pop, will you tuck me in?" the kids begged their grandfather.

"Of course, my little tale travellers."

The house became quiet, everyone fell asleep, even the chickens in the yard, who didn't even know that they had a three-headed cousin.

Day Nine

The kids came down from upstairs, yawning. They didn't really want to have breakfast either. Mum and Pop begged them to eat.

"Pop, is there a cave nearby?" asked Pete.

"Cave? No there isn't one, but there is a smaller grot, carved out by water at the place we are going today. It's not far from Tutelage Rock.

"Tutelage?" asked Judy. "What a strange name! Will we go there too?"

"If you want to..."

"Of course!" they shouted in unison.

"Then eat your breakfast."

They needed nothing else. They began stuffing themselves, gobbling down everything so that they could get on the road as quickly as possible. When they got out of the car, they had to walk another twenty minutes. They started to get a bit grumpy, but then, after the next turn, they saw the rock. It was tall and took up the entire hillside. The rock face was almost entirely vertical, with the top two edges widening. Papa explained that the name Tutelage Rock came from the fact that it resembled someone holding out two hands for protection. It was very popular among rock climbers, and many people were attempting to reach the top while they were talking.

"Pop, aren't they afraid they will fall down?" asked Judy in a hushed voice.

"They probably are, a little bit."

"Then why are they doing it?"

"Because it's a good feeling, overcoming your fears and knowing you achieved something."

They were looking at the climbers for a long time. They listened in awe as the carabiners clanged, and the pebbles reeled back. Then the kids turned to Pop and asked him to show them the cave. They walked a little bit through the woods; the two sides of the ravine were steep, and there was a grot in one of the rocks.

"There's the cave!" they shouted and started running.

The cave was a hollow, carved out by water. When they screamed, their voices echoed. The kids really liked it. They shouted things like, "I am the caveman! And be aware bears!"

When they shouted for a while, giggling at the echoes, they went home. The kids continued playing in the garden. Mum told Pop that she would make lunch.

"Make toad in the hole."

"Pop, you know they never eat that."

"Try it, maybe now they will. You could use the sausage Tom gave us."

"Really, Uncle Tom, I remember him. How old is he?"

"He will be eighty-eight, but he still making his own smoked sausages."

Mum made the toad in the hole with little enthusiasm, but it smelled great. She was ready to make something else for the children. But as soon as they sat down at the table, they exclaimed, „It smells delicious!" and dug in. Mum was very happy. There really must be something in that country air.

The afternoon passed, and it was getting dark. It took some time, but they persuaded Pete and Judy to bathe. When they returned from the bathroom, Pop was already waiting for them.

"Now, travellers, are we going to the land of stories for a journey?"

“Traveller Pete wants to, he is ready for the tale!”

“Traveller Judy is ready for the tale!”

“Then I will join too. Traveller Mum is ready for the tale.”

There was only the countdown left.

“10, 9, 8, 7, 6, 5, 4, 3, 2, 1, and... 0!” they chanted together.

“And so the ninth story begins...”

The Cowardly Knight

The king of the Kingdom of Tutelage ascended the throne at a young age. His uncle did not like the fact that a boy was running the country. So he seized every opportunity to depose the throne through trickery or to pull the strings from the background. It appeared that luck was also on his side, as the young Vladimir enjoyed mingling with his people dressed in camouflage.

When he went to the fair in his ripped clothes, no one recognised him. Not even the pretty girl selling yarn, though the king had spoken with her before. He was trying to court her, but she laughed and hit him with a ball of yarn.

"Tell me now, do you have a suitor?" asked Vladimir.

"Why would I have one? Well, many joke about courting me, but where I live, people are poor, and it costs a lot of money."

"Okay, but do you fancy anyone?"

"Oh, leave me alone with these stupid questions," she said.

"And what if the king asked for your hand?"

"You idiot!" laughed the girl. "He doesn't want to marry a poor girl. He has a hundred princesses and duchesses in his court who are more beautiful and cultured. He'll find a lady for himself there."

They began all of their conversations this way, and then they noticed that the market was emptying out, and they were still just talking to each other, becoming lost in each other's eyes. The king finally had enough. He told her he was the king, and that he loved her and wanted to marry her. She, well, she had a name; her name was Judith. She did not believe him, but he took a golden ducat with his image on it.

The yarn-seller girl could not believe her eyes. Then she became enraged and told Vladimir not to mess with her; she was not the type of girl to be swept off her feet with a few nice words, so she ran away. But she was that kind of girl, she just had to admit that to herself. She did eventually. Of course, she did not want to run away because she adored him, but she was desperate because she was not cut out to be queen. Such a poor girl could never be the king's wife. Such things only happened in fairy tales she had heard as a child.

And Vladimir set out in great sorrow, but instead of going to the palace, he went to a poor neighbourhood. Just then, the commander of the army, who had been following him for a long time, stepped up to him and snapped at him.

"Stop, you good-for-nothing, where are you going at this late hour?"

"How dare you speak to your king this way, you bold soldier? Watch your mouth!"

The soldier needed nothing more, so he searched his pockets for the golden ducat, as instructed by Vladimir's uncle. He accused him of stealing it, tied him up, and took him to the dungeon. The uncle sat there, rubbing his hands with satisfaction.

"Oh, dumb little Vladimir! Now I've outsmarted you."

It happened that, a travelling circus came to the country, and one of the performers resembled Vladimir. Well, only from a distance, but that was enough for the uncle to bring him to the palace to pretend to be the king.

Those in the court witnessed the exchange, but they were threatened that if they opened their mouths, their heads would be severed from their bodies, making living in such conditions extremely uncomfortable.

Meanwhile, Gerhard Wallenberg, a glorious knight, or the sad-faced knight, as he referred to himself, though anyone who looked at him would interpret it differently, as most people laughed at him because he always had such a funny expression. So Gerhard Wallenberg was on his way to his quarters, almost sad-faced. Outside the inn stood a soldier.

"If your life is dear to you, you will leave me, for I am the famous sad-faced knight, Gerhard Wallenberg," he said loudly.

"Well, don't go to a funeral, or the mourners will laugh when they see you," the soldier praised him.

And he burst out laughing so hard that he could hardly stop.

"But I will let you in, because I'm in a good mood now."

As Gerhard entered his room, he cursed his parents for passing on such traits to him. But at that moment, he screamed so loudly that a customer in the restaurant swallowed the fried meat whole in shock. The cause of the yelling was a mouse that had been happily munching away in his room. But the sad-faced knight was so terrified of everything that he stood frozen until the mouse gave him a disapproving look and exited the room.

Gerhard was devastated and wept quietly, wondering why he was such a coward. Climbing the wall used to be his favourite pastime, but when he looked down once, he was terrified of the height and nearly fell. Since then, he has only rented a room on the ground floor.

Judith had been waiting for days for the king to show up. She might have left him hanging, but she still liked him a lot. She cursed herself for running away, but

to no avail; Vladimir never showed up again. Then, one day at the market, she heard from the other vendors the rumour that he had been arrested. The girl had had enough, and she became frantic. The others realised something was wrong, that it was not just pity, and that there was more to it. They advised her to look up a knight who lived nearby, as he might be able to help.

She wandered the streets, asking around, until she found the knight. She entered his room, looked at him, and then turned back. But she was so desperate that she went back to the knight.

"Are you the knight?" she asked, holding back her laughter.

"I am at your service, the sad-faced knight! Gerhard Wallenberg!"

"Forgive me, I am deeply distressed," said Judith, laughing.

"Yes, I see. If you are distressed now, what must you be like when you are sad?"

But the girl burst into tears as she remembered the face of the dear boy, I mean the king, who was now rotting in the dungeon. The knight was taken aback and inquired as to what was wrong, as he had never seen anyone cry in front of him before.

The yarn-seller girl told the entire story, claiming that he had been recommended as the one who could free the king.

"No," said the sad-faced knight, turning down the opportunity, "I'm not going up there. I'm afraid of heights!"

"My dear knight, only you can help me."

She pleaded for quite a long time, but to no avail. Finally, she angrily threatened the knight with several large slaps on the face if he refused to help. However, it was the girl's angry and piercing gaze that convinced him to climb the tower. The working life had hardened the girl after all. And the saying goes: love conquers all. They set out after dark for the tower, but two highwaymen blocked their path. They were highwaymen, after all. One of them asked them for money in a low voice.

"Listen," said the knight. "Let's not play games with each other. Do I look like someone who has money? But if you help me, everyone will have money. We just have to get the king out of jail."

This convinced two highwaymen to go with them as travelling companions, for they were travelling for a long time after that. They had no battle plan, but they were not soldiers – except for the sad-faced knight – though it would have been hard to win a battle with him anyway. As they approached the dungeon, the two highwaymen began to raise their voices. The guards came out to chase them away, but they held the guards down and tied them up. The sad-faced knight stepped up to the tower, which was at least a hundred feet tall.

"He's surely not up there, is he? I won't go up there, never in a million years. I'd rather be cut in four."

Then he changed his mind after the two highwaymen marked lines for the cutting on his body and drew a rather sharp sword.

"Only because you asked so nicely."

With trembling legs, he took out nails and hooks, and while the highwaymen lifted him up to where the bricks began, he drove the first one into the tower's wall. He took out a rope and began climbing. And as the girl watched from below, smiling, Gerhard Wallenberg kept telling himself:

"Just don't look down, okay? Please, don't look down! This tower is not high, oh no."

Of course, he looked down and was so frightened that he almost let go of the rope.

"Holy Father, just save me this time!" he cried. "I won't swear anymore. And I won't eat sweets. Well, only sometimes. Just don't let me fall off, okay? You need me. I need me for sure, I'm used to being."

He did not fall because, despite his numerous flaws, Gerhard was one of the best wall climbers. He did not even fall when a mouse crawled out of a hole and onto his hand. He did not fall, but it occurred to him that he would rather throw himself into the deep than have the furry thing stick to him. The mouse gave him a scornful look before returning to the crack.

The sad-faced knight eventually made his way up to the king. He used a chisel to pry the window bars open, and together they were able to get it out. Now they only had to bring the king down. Only! They tied a safety rope around his waist and began climbing down. And, miraculously, the knight was so focused on protecting the king that he forgot to be afraid. When they got down, the girl threw herself into the boy-king's arms, getting his shirt quite wet. So they were happy.

Now they only needed to get into the palace. Since the wall-climbing went so well, the king and knight climbed this wall as well, while the two highwaymen outside distracted the guards. They entered through the window of the uncle's bedroom. The uncle turned pale, unable even to laugh at the sad-faced knight. The king summoned the guards and imprisoned his uncle as well as the actor hired to fill in for him.

Then he summoned the yarn-seller girl and asked her again whether she wanted to be the king's wife or not. Of course she did. They had a grand wedding. The two highwaymen were appointed commanders of the guard and were well compensated. Gerhard Wallenberg was awarded the title of the King's bravest knight. He stopped calling himself the sad-faced knight. He even kept a mouse in his house.

Pop finished the story. Mum laughed because she knew that the Kingdom of Tutelage got its name from the rock. The kids were asking questions about the tower climbing they had seen at the cliff this morning. They didn't forget to ask Pop for a repeat. By the time he got to the end of the tale again, they were blinking heavily and were barely awake.

Mum tucked them in, and then she went out into the garden to Pop, and they watched the stars in silence.

"The weather will be nice tomorrow," Pop said, looking at the sky.

"You can tell it from the stars?"

"Yes, if the stars are twinkling the weather won't change. And they are twinkling right now."

"Really, I've just remembered," smiled Mum. "You told me when I was a kid."

"It is great, having you here. I was waiting for so long to have a holiday together. And now here we are! We did it. I think Pete and Judy is also having a great time."

"They surely do."

They listened to the crickets chirping and watched the bats fly after that, but then everything went quiet. Mum and Pop talked for a long time. That was the final night; the holiday will end tomorrow. They will return home, and the family will reunite once Dad has come home from work.

Day Ten

As the sun tickled the children's cheeks, their eyes opened instantly. They washed their faces and dressed, then dashed to the kitchen. They were laughing as their feet drummed against the stairs. The table was covered in pancakes, maple syrup, eggs, sausages, beans, and bacon. Mum was not surprised when the kids ate well, talked the entire time, and asked Pop about their plans for the day.

"Today we will take a ship to an island, and we will spend almost the full day there."

"And will we eat there?" asked Pete.

"Yes, there's a firepit and a stewing pot. We will make Irish stew with Mum while you play."

"Do we like that?" asked Judy.

"They don't," whispered Mum to Pop. "They've never finished it."

"They will if there is nothing else," shrugged his shoulders Pop.

He was already packing the ingredients; he also packed fresh bread.

„Okay, Dad, but you'll be responsible if they come back hungry," said Mum.

The ship had a gentle wind, and the children clung to the railing, enjoying the breeze in their hair. They soon arrived at Mosquito Island, as Pop called it. There were numerous small hatches leading into the water designed for fishermen, but no one was using them. They spotted a small lookout in the middle of the reeds. They nagged Pop to go there, but he wanted to go anyway; he did not need to be convinced. A long wooden path led to the lookout. It was not high, just high enough to reach over the reeds. They used binoculars to observe the ducks, swans, and various other birds. The water below was alive with tadpoles, small fish, and frogs. A stork flew overhead, so close that they could almost touch it. They watched for a while before returning to the island to play. Pop and Mum prepared the stew, Pop lit a fire, and the food was soon cooking, smelling delicious all around. When the children smelled it, they ran back to the fire. They sat around the wooden table, Mum took the food out into plastic bowls they brought from home, and Pop took out the bread. Mum could not believe her eyes when she saw her children, the little ones who hated stew, devouring the food.

"Dad, pinch me," said Mom. "If I didn't see this with my own eyes, I definitely wouldn't believe it."

"Come on! They were hungry, there was nothing else to eat."

But Mum wasn't so sure. In the afternoon, the ship came, and they went home. Mum and the two kids packed their bags because they had to go home.

"You know, Dad, I didn't think the holiday would go so well. It would be nice to spend longer weekends together more frequently. You are a fantastic influence on the children. They really liked everything here."

When it was time to say goodbye, one by one they ran up to Pop, hugged him, and whispered, "I love you, Pop."

Then Mum started the engine, and they drove home. They didn't talk on the way. They were thinking of the holiday and the stories.

In the evening, after bath time, they climbed into their familiar beds. Pete and Judy looked at Mum questioningly.

"Now I will tell you a story, but we can't skip the report," smiled Mum.

"Traveller Pete is ready for the tale!" said Pete, laughing.

"Traveller Judy is ready for the tale!" chuckled Judy.
Mum stopped for a moment then said it too:
"Traveller Mum is ready for the tale!"
There was only the countdown left.
"10, 9, 8, 7, 6, 5, 4, 3, 2, 1 and... 0!" they shouted in unison.
"And so the tenth story begins..."

Pirates

Leopold Wolfgang was sitting on the riverbank and crying. As a grown man, he was a little ashamed of being emotional. He was a well-built, muscular young lad with blond hair and grey eyes. Everyone thought he was handsome, so it was surprising to see him cry so hard. But only to those who did not know the reason, and Leopold did. He had been a cook, preparing lunch in a restaurant, but the customers who had tried it were now after him. The food was so bad that they were furious and threatened him with terrible vengeance if he was caught. So, instead of fleeing, he was crying, but it was only because of the peeled onion, not because of the crowd looking for him. He had not washed his hands and had forgotten not to rub his face. So he cleansed his eyes eagerly, and when the pain subsided, he put on his shoes and began walking with a strange hopping motion. He would have continued on his way if he had not been stopped by an elderly man with a beard and a leather eye patch over one eye, who looked like a pirate.

"Where to, where to, young man with such strange footprints?"

"Oh, is this what you're talking about?" looked Leopold back. "I put a horseshoe on my shoe to cover the tracks."

"But why are the horseshoes on backwards?"

"Because it makes it look like I'm going when I'm coming."

The captain, as he was a captain after all, thought about it for a moment, pulling up the eye patch to get a better look at the tracks.

"You're not half blind?" Leopold gaped. "Then why are you wearing the eye patch?"

"It gives me more authority. You know what they say: A one-eyed man is king in the land of pirates."

"I only heard the saying that the one-eyed man is king in the land of the blind."

"Whatever, that's irrelevant now," and he pulled back the leather eye patch.

"Haven't you been wearing it on the other eye?"

"Thanks, sometimes I forget. Can you tell me why you have horseshoes on your feet?"

"Do you want the longer or shorter version?"

"I'd prefer the short one."

Leopold explained that he worked in a restaurant and was being chased by some customers. He thought he would only mention in the longer version that the reason was because of his bad cooking, but why brag about it if you don't have to.

"Well, then you've met the right man," the pirate captain concluded. "If you want, I'll take you aboard my ship."

"I'd even consider being a dancer now, so I'll take you up on that deal," Leopold kept looking back, becoming more and more nervous.

So the deal was done. He took off his horseshoes and hurried after the captain, who led him with surprising speed into the harbour. They boarded the ship and as if they were only waiting for him, they set sail. The truth is that they were actually waiting for him because the captain was looking for a cook to replace the previous one, who had grown old and retired.

Leopold entered the kitchen, jumped up and down with enthusiasm, and dinner was soon ready. The next day, the captain summoned him and yelled at him, somewhat angrily.

"Why didn't you tell me you can't cook?"

"That was in the longer version, but you asked for the shorter."

"I'm about to have a stroke! What am I going to do with you now?" the pirate glared angrily at the lad, his eye patch pulled up over his forehead. "You'll work on deck from today. Understood?"

"I understand. But I think you'd better adjust that eye patch, because you've got it on the wrong side again."

And so began his life among the pirates, who were relieved to learn that he was no longer cooking and eventually grew to like him for it. And for other reasons. Because he climbed the masts as skilfully as if he'd been doing it all his life. He scrubbed the decks, washed the rail, was never tired, and in the evenings he sang mournful songs to the savage sailors, making many of them cry, because his voice was quite good, and they were sentient souls beneath the grim appearance. For music, that is.

On the deck, Leopold's skin was tanned a golden brown, his blond hair even lighter in the sun, and his grey eyes were in a striking contrast with his face. Any girl could easily fall for him. When he finished his day's work, the pirates taught him how to fight and defend himself when he encountered enemies. Eventually, he came to like the pirates.

One day, when they were near land, the captain called for him.

"My dear boy," he said, then repeated it because he liked the sound of it. "My dear boy, we are about to moor. You have earned your money. I will give you ten gold coins and a whistle."

"A whistle?" said Leopold, surprised. "What will I do with a whistle?"

"If you get in trouble, just blow it. I'll somehow find out you used it and come to your rescue."

Leopold thanked him for helping him escape from his chasers and giving shelter on the boat. The captain hugged him and made him promise never to enter a kitchen again, and the handsome man, because he was really a man by now, agreed. He walked towards the town, and the captain gave the order to set sail, adjusting his eye patch slightly so they would not notice he was getting emotional.

Leopold caused quite a stir in town because he had truly matured into a handsome lad, a man. He didn't stop until he reached the square in front of the royal palace. He kept turning his head, for he had never seen such sad people. But he asked them in vain, and they didn't say why their faces were so sad. He stayed at the inn the next day and ate breakfast, which was delicious and far superior to anything he had ever cooked in the kitchen. So while he was eating, he heard that they were looking for a gardener for the royal court. He thought he could certainly do it, so he applied. When they saw him, they realised that with muscles like his, the job would be easy, so they handed him a scythe and sent him to work in the vast field behind the palace tower. Of course, every king has a beautiful daughter, and King Ottokar was no exception, but he had already promised her hand to the Duke of Lombardy, as is customary among kings.

The princess was devastated, especially when she looked out the window and saw Leopold, who had removed his shirt in the heat and was cutting the grass with steady, smooth movements. Who could this lad be? The princess wondered, then moved closer to the window and accidentally dropped her handkerchief, so she had to run out behind the tower. She happened to be quite taken with the lad, who, not by accident, did not even look at her because he was too busy cutting the grass. The princess was annoyed because she was used to noble men complimenting her in order to gain her favour. Who could this

servant be who would not even look at her? Who could this handsome lad be that would ignore her? Who is this fantastically charming, tanned, muscular, and attractive man with steel-blue eyes that she cannot stop thinking about? Such thoughts raced through her mind, and she eventually could not take it any longer and returned to the garden to learn everything she could about him. But near him, she forgot what she wanted, could not speak, and her heart was racing. After a while, Leopold noticed the girl in her pretty dress. He then noticed that she was a very beautiful girl. When he got to this point, he stopped mowing and said to her cheekily:

"Hello, it's hot, isn't it? I'm quite hot. Can you pass me my bottle?"

The princess didn't even know what she was doing, so she threw it, but as soon as he caught it, she suddenly realised what she had done and made a very angry face.

"Who do you think you are? I am the princess."

"I am Leopold Wolfgang, gardener and honorary pirate," he bowed, the title of cook better left unmentioned.

The princess began to laugh because this introduction seemed so out of place. They ended up laughing together. They walked a little in the garden, then a lot more, and she did not even notice, but she liked this charming lad even more, if that is possible. Later, Leopold sang to her, but then she blushed, because liking him was a mild way of saying what she felt. Later, she wondered if it was his muscular tanned body, his grey eyes, his beautiful voice, or all of them combined, but she was drawn to him. The next day, she went down to the garden, followed by the third day, afternoon, and evening. At night, she realised she had fallen in love with this man, which was impossible given that she was to marry the Duke of Lombardy in a week. She had no idea what to do; she liked this guy and that was it, and she did not want to go to Lombardy. But

she knew she must forget Leopold, for there could never
be anything between them, for he was only a gardener.
But what a gardener! And that was the problem.

It was no coincidence that the people of King Ottokar's
country were in a bad mood because the neighbouring
kingdom threatened them and eventually declared war on
him. This kingdom was significantly larger than King Ottokar's kingdom of Mosquitoaria. They had a large army that
conquered more and more of the king's territory. When
King Ottokar learned they were losing the war, he became
extremely depressed. The only way the King of Lombardy
would was through the marriage, but his daughter was

stalling, which was understandable. Ottokar called his daughter to him.

"You will tell the Duke of Lombardy at once that you are going to marry him, and I will not have any objection!" said the king, broken-hearted.

In despair, the princess informed Leopold that she had been forced to marry the heir to the throne of Lombardy. That was all the lad needed, as he had already fallen deeply in love with this sincere princess.

He paced, grumbled, argued with himself, and eventually blew the whistle. Of course, nothing happened; blowing the whistle like that is only effective in fairy tales. So he went to bed and fell asleep in despair. The sun was already up when he heard a loud noise. As he blinked the sleep from his eyes, the pirate captain appeared before him. A seagull had heard the whistle and flown to the ship, pecking at the captain's cap until he sailed to shore, and the bird guided them here. Leopold began smiling; the whistle was useful after all. He quickly explained what was going on, and the captain organised his men into battle formation, surprising the neighbouring kingdom's army with unexpected pirate attacks. They fought so well that the enemy eventually retreated and returned to their home country. Everyone in the palace was overjoyed. The king had to summon Leopold, but when he saw the well-dressed lad, he only said this:

"Wow!" and he even whistled. "I want beautiful grand-children, that's all."

"My king, may I marry your daughter?" asked the shocked lad.

But the king had long since softened and said yes because of their victory in battle.

Leopold hosted a lavish feast, to which the pirates were of course invited. And, for the first time in history, the royal guard consisted of large, burly pirates. No one

dared to argue with them, and even their enemies avoided them. The kingdom prospered, and Leopold and Catherine blessed King Ottokar with lovely grandchildren, and he did not regret having such a handsome son-in-law.

"Repeat it, please!" said Judy.
Then, when Mum did, Pete laughed.
"This story is similar to the ones Pop told."
"Why? Am I not similar to Pop?"
"You are," chuckled Pete.

They talked a bit about the pirates and the sails and even recalled a few things that happened when they were at Pop's. Then they dozed off.

Mum called up Pop and told him the story she told the kids. Pop also liked the tale, and he was happy that they enjoyed the holiday. They talked for a while, then Mum hanged up.

She smiled as she thought of the last ten days. Dad will come home tomorrow, they will have a lot to tell him. But that's another story.